THE
LIVING CHURCH

Scriptural Principles for Building a Vibrant Church

AYORINDE IDOWU

The Living Church

Scriptural Principles for Building a Vibrant Church

Copyright © 2019 by **Ayorinde Idowu**

ISBN: 978-1-944652-86-9

Printed in the United States of America. All rights reserved solely by the publisher. This book or parts thereof may not be reproduced in any form, stored in a retrieval system, or transmitted in any form by any means - electronic, mechanical, photocopy. Unless otherwise noted, Bible quotations are taken from the Holy Bible, New King James Version. Copyright 1982 by Thomas Nelson, Inc., publishers. Used by permission.

Published By:
Cornerstone Publishing
A division of Cornerstone Creativity Group LLC
Info@thecornerstonepublishers.com
www.thecornerstonepublishers.com

Author's Information
To contact the author or to order copies of the book, please call (281)-989-2208 or email: Ayorinde_idowu@hotmail.com

CONTENTS

Dedication..7
Acknowledgments...9
Introduction..11

Chapter 1
God's Dwelling-Place..13

Chapter 2
Motivating Church Members.....................................31

Chapter 3
Small Groups: Purpose And Pattern...........................61

Chapter 4
Small Groups: Impacts And Leadership......................77

Chapter 5
Kingdom Workers' Accountability.............................97

Chapter 6
Christ's Resurrection And The Church.....................107

Chapter 7
The Price of Our Redemption..................123

Chapter 8
Power in the Name Of Jesus....................133

Chapter 9
Foundation of True Success.....................147

Chapter 10
Fasting That Works....................................159

Chapter 11
Necessity of True Repentance..................171

Chapter 12
Life's Inescapable Storms And God's Faithfulness..181

List of References..190

DEDICATION

To all members of the true Church of the living God worldwide.

ACKNOWLEDGMENTS

I appreciate and thank the various spiritual groups at Living Word Chapel for their interactive fellowship, and the support received from the three generations of my family base here in Houston, Texas, USA.

INTRODUCTION

So much has happened since Christ made the powerfully prophetic pronouncement, "...Upon this rock I will build my church; and the gates of hell shall not prevail against it" (Matthew 16:18, KJV). The church has indeed been established with great power and authority on the earth. And in the course of time, it has penetrated virtually every nook and cranny of the world, with local gatherings of believers from every tongue and tribe springing up, worshipping God, influencing their cultures and advancing the Kingdom.

There are at least three fundamental revelations from this declaration of our Lord that should be of interest to us individually and in our local gatherings. One is that the church will be built, not dropped from heaven. This means that the growth and development of the church into what God desires it to be will be a progressive process that requires diligence, patience, perseverance and steadfastness. Second is that Christ Himself must be the principal engineer of the building, which means that nothing can be done without His leading, counsel and power; otherwise our labors will not be recognized in heaven.

Lastly, the declaration reveals to us that the church of Christ is a triumphant gathering. It is one that the gates of hell can never prevail against. This triumph is all-encompassing. It is triumph over sin, Satan, sickness, afflictions, limitations, oppressions, oppositions and persecutions. Simply put, the church that Christ has in mind is one that is unstoppable in flourishing spiritually and numerically – one that is enforcing the will of God on the earth, exercising unlimited authority and dominion, frustrating and paralyzing the activities of the forces of darkness, liberating the captives of the evil one, while at the same time keeping itself undefiled, undivided and ever ready for the coming of the Bridegroom.

How do we attain this glorious standard that has been set for us? The comprehensive guidelines, as laid down in the Scriptures, are what you will find in this book. As you read through, prayerfully and meditatively, you will discover the proven principles for working with Christ, the Master Builder, in building your life and your church for unlimited victory. You will also discover doctrines and directions that will guide you in effectively shepherding your church, maximizing its potentials and fortifying it against internal failings and external onslaughts. Now is the time to move on to greater heights!

Chapter 1

GOD'S DWELLING-PLACE

"The church is not wood and stone, but the company of people who believe in Christ" - MARTIN LUTHER

It was a quite spectacular evening, one that would not be forgotten for eternity. The sun had long set, far to the west over the Mediterranean. All of nature, to use the words of J.R Miller, was hushed to restfulness - nothing could be heard but the rippling streams; and nothing could be seen but the pale silvery moonlight, falling on the scenic snows of the mountain. Up there in the sky, multitudes of stars shone like temple lamps lit in the outer court of some magnificent sanctuary.

Kneeling on the peak of the mountain was Jesus in deep supplication to God. Not very far from Him were three of His disciples, whom He had taken along as fellow watchers in prayer but whom were now fast asleep from the day's fatigue. Suddenly, the appearance of the kneeling Messiah took a majestically glorious form, the brightness of which temporarily overshadowed the glow of the stars above. Almost at the same time, two glorified beings – Moses and Elijah -appeared on either side of Jesus, and the three soon began to converse.

Apparently roused from their slumber by the blinding lights around them, the disciples awoke with a start and naturally wondered whether they were in a trance or simply imagining things. When they eventually realized what was going on, they were filled with such wonder and euphoria that Peter impulsively exclaimed, "Master, it is good for us to be here; and let us make three tabernacles: one for You, one for Moses, and one for Elijah"—not knowing what he said." But there was more to come; for soon, the Shekinah glory itself descended from heaven, with the voice of God saying, "This is my beloved Son, in whom I am well pleased; hear him."

Afterward, it was soon time to come down from the mountain, to return to the realities of daily living. And it didn't take long for these realities to resume, for just as Jesus and the disciples were descending the mountain, a man brought a seemingly hopeless case for him to handle. And so, it was that the Messiah and the disciples who had just beheld the glory of God and heard His voice now had to contend with the sight and screams of a demon-possessed boy and his desperate father (See Luke 9:28-42).

PARALLEL EXPERIENCE

I related the above account so as to compare it with the feeling that we often experience when we have been at a church, a revival program, or a retreat where we have been tremendously blessed spiritually. Just like Peter, we get this "feeling" that we are covered in glory on the outside and brimming with peace and joy on the inside. But then, soon after leaving the gathering, all the excitement seems to vanish immediately, as if we had just descended a glowing mountain peak into a deep, dark valley of emptiness.

This often brings doubts and confusion to our hearts because the number one desire of all true believers is to have an intimate and uninterrupted connection with our heavenly Father. Accordingly, we treasure every moment we get this sense of closeness to Him. The challenge however is that these moments, for many, are often inconsistent, appearing when least expected and going when most needed.

For this reason, many of us, just like Peter, sometimes find ourselves wishing not to depart from the church

The Living Church

premises or any similar place of gathering. Some of us even wish to be transformed into something like the church building itself or the Old Testament's Ark of Covenant. We may even wish that we are already taken to heaven, so as not to have a single moment without feeling the infinitely pleasant and refreshing presence of God.

Yet, in all of these, there are two established truths that we are overlooking. The first is that we do not necessarily need to be in a church building or gathering for us to feel the presence of God. The desire of God for every New Testament believer is for us to be His very temple – to carry and feel Him in the fullness of His glory, power and majesty everywhere we go. 1 Corinthians 3:16 says, "Do you not know that you are the temple of God and that the Spirit of God dwells in you?"

The second truth is that in the conflict of feelings that we get between when we are in a place of fellowship with other believers and when we are on our own outside of it is a way of God passing a fundamental message to each one of us: "I do not live in the church; I live in your heart. I want you to realize this truth. I am a person and I want you to know Me and have a personal relationship with Me. Because I love you, I created you so that you could experience my love and love Me in return. "Since you were precious in

My sight, You have been honored, And I have loved you; Therefore I will give men for you, And people for your life (Isaiah 43:4)."

CALL TO SANCTITY

This certainty of our being God's new dwelling-place is confirmed and emphasized by His repeated calls to us to treat our bodies with sanctity and keep it in holiness at all times. This is similar to the way the architectural temple of God was often treated in the Old Testament, and is also a reflection of how most of us still handle our physical places of fellowship today. In 1 Corinthians 3, where we read earlier, it says, "Do you not know that you are the temple of God and that the Spirit of God dwells in you? If anyone defiles the temple of God, God will destroy him. For the temple of God is holy, which temple you are" (16-17).

Also, 1 Corinthians 6:18-20 says, "Flee sexual immorality. Every sin that a man does is outside the body, but he who commits sexual immorality sins against his own body. Or do you not know that your body is the temple of the Holy Spirit who is in you, whom you have from God, and you are not your own? For you were bought at a price; therefore glorify God in your body and in your spirit, which are God's."

The Living Church

Paul called on the Corinthians, who apparently had a weakness for sexual immorality, to have self-awareness about the ultimate identity of their corporate body. They were a temple built by God. Sexual immorality is unique among sins insomuch as it is a sin against the body, thus assaulting the sanctity of a believer's sacred oneness with Christ (sealed by the Holy Spirit in you) and the oneness of holy matrimony (1 Corinthians 7:12).

The ultimate message is that the believer's body is a sacred vessel, bought at a huge price by the Son of God. Believers thus have no business doing anything with the Lord's temple that does not glorify Him.

Basically, therefore, having been confirmed to be God's very dwelling-place, we are all the things that we ever wished to be - and even more. 1 Corinthians 12:27 says, "Now you are the body of Christ, and members individually."

In response to a question on how to keep ourselves in this communion with God, Jesus answers, "If anyone loves Me, he will keep My word; and My Father will love him, and We will come to him and make Our home with him" (John 14:23). What this means is that while Jesus wants to come to us, it is not automatic that He will come and make His home with us. We have to invite Him in. In Revelation 3:20, He says, "Behold,

I stand at the door and knock. If anyone hears My voice and opens the door, I will come in to him and dine with him, and he with Me."

This is the starting point of this communion. To maintain it, however, we have a distinct requirement, "If anyone loves Me, he will keep My word…" We must devote ourselves to studying, meditating on and abiding by God's word for us to be in constant communion with the Holy Trinity.

HISTORICAL INSIGHTS ON THE CHURCH

Let's return to our discussion on the real meaning of the church and get further insights. It is quite common that at the mention of the word "church", the immediate picture that springs up in the minds of most people is that of a building with either a simple or fancy architectural structure where believers gather. Some also see the church as the name of a particular Christian denomination. The truth, however, is that the church is much more than these in biblical terms. In fact, the church, in its original meaning, has nothing to do with buildings but all about people.

The branch of theology that seeks to understand all aspects of the church is known as *"ecclesiology"*, a term derived from the Greek word *"ekklesia"*, generally referring to a gathering or an assembly. The early

THE LIVING CHURCH

Christian church had no buildings. Since they were often persecuted, they usually met to fellowship in secret homes. However, as the influence of Christianity spread, buildings were erected for believers to worship and fellowship in groups. This trend eventually transformed extensively into what we presently call churches, synagogues, or cathedrals.

It goes without saying, therefore, that the church consists of people, not buildings. People are responsible to conduct fellowship, worship and ministry, not buildings. Church structures do not fulfill the role of God's people, but simply facilitate their functions. J. Philpot has well noted that "The New Testament never, in any one instance, means, by "the house of God," any material building." Explaining this further, Mark Dever, in the book, "Nine Marks of a Healthy Church", says: "The church is primarily a body of people who profess and give evidence that they have been saved by God's grace alone, for His glory alone, through faith alone, in Christ alone. This is what a New Testament church is; it is not a building. The early Christians didn't have buildings for almost 300 years after the church began. The collection of people committed to Christ in a local area constitutes a church."

IDENTITY OF THE CHURCH

Essentially, the church is the community of faithful believers under the headship of Jesus Christ. Colossians 1:18 states, "And He is the head of the body, the church, who is the beginning, the firstborn from the dead, that in all things He may have the preeminence." Here, Paul uses "head" in two senses. One is to imply authority, rule, and supreme rank (see also Colossians 2:10,19); it plays on the imagery of Christ's relationship to the church as head of the body (1 Corinthians 12:12-27; Ephesians 1:22; 4:5; 5:23). Secondly, Christ is the head because He is the beginning and the firstborn from the dead. This parallel language to creation identifies the church as part of the new creation that was inaugurated with the resurrection of Christ. His res I appreciate and thank the various spiritual groups at Living Word Chapel for their interactive fellowship, and the support received from the three generations of my family base here in Houston, Texas, USA urrection resulted in the fulfillment of God's purpose for Christ, giving Him preeminence.

The church comprises those who have been called out of the world. 1 Peter 2:9 describes them as "a chosen generation, a royal priesthood, a holy nation, His own special people, that you may proclaim the praises of Him who called you out of darkness into His marvelous light." The phrase "chosen generation"

The Living Church

(also used in Isaiah 43:20) refers to the corporate unity of believers. In Christ, believers of all races are unified as one people. They are a royal priesthood – a collective company of priests who offer up spiritual sacrifices to God (1 Peter 2:5).

The church is the body of Christ whose members are filled with the Holy Spirit, as emphasized by the Bible. 1 Corinthians 12:27-28 reveals, "Now you are the body of Christ, and members individually. And God has appointed these in the church: first apostles, second prophets, third teachers, after that miracles, then gifts of healings, helps, administrations, varieties of tongues." The church refers to not just to the local body of believers at Corinth, but to the universal church, composed of all believers everywhere and from every age. This means that the true church is beyond denominationalism.

In Acts 1:8, Jesus promised the disciples, "But you shall receive power when the Holy Spirit has come upon you; and you shall be witnesses to Me in Jerusalem, and in all Judea and Samaria, and to the end of the earth." The major focus of the book of Acts is stated in this verse. First, the empowering presence is to be the Holy Spirit, not Jesus Himself. Jesus prepared His disciples for the transition, when the Holy Spirit would come to be a constant presence in His bodily absence. Second, the growth of the church would emerge through the witness of the disciples. The church is identified as a community that actively witnesses their faith in Jesus Christ right from the beginning. Third, the result of the witnessing would be remarkable, progressive, global growth.

The growth would commence in Jerusalem, then spread in concentric circles to other Jewish areas, including Judea; edges of Judaism, including Samaria; and eventually the Roman Empire. The church envisioned that it must keep expanding its witnessing to reach the newfound "uttermost" parts, as new lands and peoples were discovered. The church intended its members to be filled with the Holy Spirit for their effectiveness, as well as caring for one another, while using their different gifts for the edification of the body.

1 Corinthians 12:25-26 says, "that there should be no schism in the body, but that the members should have the same care for one another. And if one member suffers, all the members suffer with it; or if one member is honored, all the members rejoice with it."

We clothe the private parts of the human body, which we regard as less honorable to be presented, thus according them greater honor. Similarly, God has arranged the church in such a way that the humble members are accorded greater esteem. Humility is of great value in the Kingdom of God (Matthew 18:3-4).

THE CHURCH AT A GLANCE

- We believers are the church of God in the New Testament.

- The church is therefore not a building or some architectural structure.

- Wherever two or three people are gathered together in the name of the Lord is a church (Matthew 18:20).

- Not all gatherings in a building are necessarily affiliated to Christ, even if they have a Christian name.

- God has given gifts and ministries to the body (Ephesians 4:11-13).

- As the body of Christ, each of us knows and manifests a part of Him (1 Corinthians 13:9); however, together, as a corporate body in unity, we know a whole lot.

- This is why if we congregate more in smaller groups (connect centers), we find it easier to go to the streets, the malls and other places with the gospel message. And collectively all of us can make bigger impacts like they did in the church of the book of Acts.

FUNCTIONS OF THE CHURCH

It has been established thus far that the church is not a building, but a body of believers with specific attributes and purposes. The visible and local church comprises the physical churches we see around us and around the world, as well as the members of these churches. The invisible and universal church, however, refers to all believers everywhere. These belong to just one church, united in Christ, not many physical churches. Everyone in the universal church is a true believer, but this is not necessarily the case with the visible and local church as it often comprises both believers and non-believers.

The biblical roles or ministries of the church adopted by a body of believers with a specific purpose to accomplish their mission and vision are foundational to it. These roles are many, but the key to any church are foundations in worship, edification, and evangelism.

Worship is God-centered and Christ-centered. This involves expressing our love by worshipping and magnifying our creator, and not about entertaining people with flashy displays or presentations. We are to praise and glorify God in worship for who He is, not just what we think we need to get in return. It is of paramount importance that every Christian partakes in regular fellowship and worship. We must recognize that God is the source and sustainer of all aspects of our lives.

Edification involves encouraging, nurturing, building up or helping believers to mature in Christ. To achieve this goal, churches have a variety of engagements such as Bible study, continuing education in related areas, discipleship, mentoring, praying for one another, hospitality and social welfare assistance.

Evangelism involves reaching out to a lost world with the Good News of Jesus Christ. Knowing the truth and being able to defend it (apologetics) is a vital role of the church, since people often have questions or doubts about Christ and Christianity. However, the church must go beyond evangelism in the sense of reaching out with the gospel to also practically demonstrating compassion and mercy by helping others. Believers must emulate Christ's example to love others; and the church, too, must make a real difference in the world, while not neglecting to share the message of Christ.

Any church that fails to fulfill any of these key foundational roles – worship, edification and evangelism - is not functioning as God intends. Whatever the challenges and struggles may be, a healthy church seeks to overcome such obstacles in a way that honors God and His intentions for His church.

IMPLICATIONS OF KNOWING WE ARE THE CHURCH

The following happens when we understand that we are truly the church of God:

1. It challenges us to honor God all the days of our lives, and not merely on Sundays or when we are within the walls of a church building. This is most favorable for us because the more we honor God, the more he blesses and manifests His power through us.

2. It totally changes our mindset, including the way we see and comport ourselves.

3. It helps us in raising our children in the way of the Lord, not only through our consistently godly lifestyle but also through our conscious decision not to abdicate our parental responsibilities to the church or the Sunday school teacher. Since we know that we are their primary "church", we make it a duty to teach them God's word at all times.

4. Current trend reveals that many church members are relinquishing the responsibility of their personal spiritual growth and the duty of reaching out to the lost, to the church. Knowing that you are the church enables you to take your destiny in your own hands, with the Holy Spirit as your teacher.

This makes you grow faster and surer, in leaps and bounds, in all ramifications.

5. It emboldens you to demonstrate the power conferred on the church everywhere you go. Jesus, in Matthew 16:19 says, "And I will give you the keys of the kingdom of heaven, and whatever you bind on earth will be bound in heaven, and whatever you loose on earth will be loosed in heaven." How marvelous would it be, for example, if you used your spiritual authority to pray for a cripple and he jumps up in a shopping mall? Oh yes, you are capable of taking the church everywhere you are! Like Peter, you can change the atmosphere wherever you are because you are a carrier of God!

LET THIS TRUTH EMPOWER YOU!

As we have seen so far, believers worldwide constitute the church and are carriers of God everywhere they are. The first century Christians lived a vibrant spiritual life, which is strongly related to their understanding of this truth. Similarly, our full realization of this truth will lead us into even more freedom with God and exploits in our communities.

The assurance from our Lord Jesus Christ Himself is "And you shall know the truth, and the truth shall make you free" (John 8:32). Now that the truth of your status as the real dwelling-place of God has been revealed to you, let it transform your thinking and lifestyle; and let it propel you into a greater dimension of effectiveness and impacts in God's Kingdom.

Chapter 2

MOTIVATING CHURCH MEMBERS

"The true shepherd spirit is an amalgam of many precious graces. He is hot with zeal, but he is not fiery with passion. He is gentle, and yet he rules his class. He is loving, but he does not wink at sin. He has power over the lambs, but he is not domineering or sharp. He has cheerfulness, but not levity; freedom, but not license; solemnity, but not gloom." - C.H. SPURGEON

From my interaction with many believers, I have realized that people value their church experiences because such experiences facilitate a spiritual outlet beneficial to human life. In addition, for many others, the church also provides a community and a sense of purpose and belonging.

Church members are encouraged to serve in the

church and support projects by enhancing this sense of community and enriching the church with social activities, as well as spiritual and service-oriented opportunities. All these actions usually inspire a strong sense of belonging, which eventually activates a higher self-esteem and a strict sense of responsibility.

To motivate is to provide with motives; to incite or impel; and most importantly, to drive or urge forward. It also means to stimulate toward action. A motive is something that causes a person to act in a certain way or do a certain thing on the goal of his or her actions, and hence constitutes the reason for the action.

EXHORTATIONS ON MEMBERSHIP MOTIVATION

Apostle Paul's exhortations on motivating church members are stated in 1 Corinthians 11:1, Acts 20:28; and 1 Timothy 4:12-16. He says in Acts 20:28, "Therefore take heed to yourselves and to all the flock, among which the Holy Spirit has made you overseers, to shepherd the church of God which He purchased with His own blood."

Paul used the language of shepherding to describe the responsibility of the leaders of the Ephesian church. He called them "overseers" (rather than elders) appointed by the Holy Spirit for their task.

Reference here to redemption through the blood of Jesus is unique in Acts, but the language reflects Paul's statements elsewhere (Romans 3:25; 5:9; Ephesians 2:13).

To Timothy, a young pastor, Paul wrote, "Let no one despise your youth, but be an example to the believers in word, in conduct, in love, in spirit, in faith, in purity. Till I come, give attention to reading, to exhortation, to doctrine. Do not neglect the gift that is in you, which was given to you by prophecy with the laying on of the hands of the eldership. Meditate on these things; give yourself entirely to them, that your progress may be evident to all. Take heed to yourself and to the doctrine. Continue in them, for in doing this you will save both yourself and those who hear you" (1 Timothy 4:12-16).

Paul asked Timothy to take heed to his ministry, to himself, and to the doctrine. "Reading" here refers to the public reading of scripture in corporate worship (see Nehemiah 8; Acts 13:15; 2 Corinthians 3:14). "Gift" refers to Timothy's calling and gifting for ministry, indicated by God (by prophecy) and recognized by the church eldership. Taken together, Paul reveals, by his exhortation to Timothy, that the most effective motivator for church members is the exemplary lifestyle of the leadership. When a leader consistently shows true Christlikeness "in word, in conduct, in love, in spirit, in faith, in purity", church members will naturally follow his or her example and the church will easily fulfill its purpose in the community.

PRINCIPLES OF MOTIVATION

Douglas McGregor, a former management professor at the Massachusetts Institute of Technology, proposed two contrasting models of motivation (known as the X and Y Theory) often applied in human resource management. A careful analysis of these models will reveal the different approaches often adopted by church leaders to shepherd their flock and the attendant results. The models are:

1. The carrot and stick model
2. The positive reinforcement model

The Carrot and Stick Model

Otherwise referred to as the reward-and-punishment model (or simply Theory X), this model thrives on the following assumptions:

- The average human being is either complacent or hates to work and would rather avoid it.
- Consequently, most people must be controlled, compelled or threatened with punishment to

make them work fully work towards achieving organizational objectives and goals. In other words, there must be certain extrinsic factors before people can be motivated towards maximum productivity.

- The average human being naturally prefers to be directed, is slow to take responsibility, has low esteem or little ambition, but ironically wants to be rewarded.

The Positive Reinforcement Model

Also known as the "intrinsic factor" model (or Theory Y), this model functions on the following assumptions:

- The average human being learns, under proper conditions, to seek responsibility, not merely because of acceptance or rewards.

- Humans exert mental and physical effort in work as naturally as they play or rest.

- When people are committed to specific and well-defined objectives, they will exercise self-control to accomplish them.

- The intellectual potential of the average human being is only partially utilized under the conditions of modern industrial practice.

- When resolving organizational problems, the capacity to demonstrate high degree of ingenuity, creativity and imagination is widely, not narrowly, distributed in the population of the workforce.

- Commitment to objectives is a function of the rewards associated with their achievement

- On the whole, this model suggests that intrinsic forces drive people to be their best.

The Y model is apparently more preferred because it is more reflective of the nature of many church members and certain to further bring out the fervency locked up in them. Ephesians 3:20-21 states, "Now to Him who is able to do exceedingly abundantly above all that we ask or think, according to the power that works in us, to Him be glory in the church by Christ Jesus to all generations, forever and ever. Amen."

Recognizing God's majestic abilities in the individual Christian and the church as a whole, Apostle Paul here prayed that God's glory would be abundantly manifested in the church; that the church would bring glory to God forever even in the eternal state.

Furthermore, Paul in Philippians 2:12-13 says, "Therefore, my beloved, as you have always obeyed, not as in my presence only, but now much more in my absence, work out your own salvation with fear and trembling; for it is God who works in you both to will and to do for His good pleasure." Here, again, the apostle emphasizes the powerful operation of the Spirit of God as the primary source of motivation within the believer. True obedience to God comes from reverence, not fright. God's works in the believer provide the deeper incentives for this. Christians are therefore recipients of God's initiatives of motivation and empowerment.

THE PASTOR AS AN EFFECTIVE MOTIVATOR

It is very important for the Pastor of the church, being the shepherd and leader of the congregation, to be wise and discerning in guiding and caring for the people under his leadership. The starting point of this is having the right perspective of the church's membership. Paul the Apostle in 2 Corinthians 5:16-17 states, "Therefore, from now on, we regard no one according to the flesh. Even though we have known Christ according to the flesh, yet now we know Him thus no longer. Therefore, if anyone is in Christ, he is a new creation; old things have passed away; behold, all things have become new."

There are always two conflicting perspectives on a situation- the natural (according to the flesh) and the divine. In the illustration given by the apostle, it was a natural view of Christ that led to His betrayal and crucifixion; and it was a similar perspective that led to Paul's previous persecution of His followers. However, after the light of divine revelation broke in on Paul on the Damascus road (Acts 9), his perspective of Christ and His followers changed drastically.

In a similar way, a Pastor who has not fully understood the peculiarity and purpose of the local church may adopt the assumptions of the Douglas McGregor's Theory X model of motivation, whereas a more discerning one will appreciate the Theory Y model. The ultimate reality, however, is that whatever understanding and perception the Pastor harbors concerning the congregation will influence the pattern of his motivation and the effectiveness of his methods.

Proverbs 23:7 says, "For as he thinks in his heart, so is he…" The inner character of church leaders definitely reflects in the way they perceive and manage the people that God has placed in their care. In Mark 11:23-24 Jesus declares, "For assuredly, I say to you, whoever says to this mountain, 'Be removed and be cast into the sea,' and does not doubt in his heart, but believes that those things he says will be done, he will have whatever he says. Therefore I say to you, whatever things you ask when you pray, believe that you receive them, and you will have them."

Here, Jesus speaks on faith and its possibilities,

and affirms the truth that our beliefs affect the manifestations that we see around us. Your basic assumptions about your church members, to a large extent, will determine your effectiveness as a dynamic motivating agent. If, for example, you see them as immature and incompetent, all you would be preoccupied with is helping to change their spiritual "diapers" all the time. On the other hand, if you choose to see them the way God sees them, it will mark a turning-point in your leadership strategy.

Giving a more realistic description of the members of the church, Paul, in Ephesians 2:10 states, "For we are His workmanship, created in Christ Jesus for good works, which God prepared beforehand that we should walk in them." The work of salvation is a display of divine workmanship. Good works are the fruit of our salvation, not the cause of it. Also, good works are not incidental to God's plan; they are, instead, an essential part of His redemption plan for each believer. Good works are demonstrated in gratitude, character, and noble actions.

KEYS TO MOTIVATING CHURCH MEMBERS

1. **Communicate vision clearly.**
Ensure that the mission and vision of your ministry are well-established and clearly understood by your

congregation. This will facilitate positive branding of the "corporate image" of your ministry.

The vision and mission of your ministry are best communicated through regular meetings in which every activity reflects these cardinal objectives. Doing this will remove ambiguities and assumptions that might create a communication gap, which could lead to frustrations and strife that are inimical to progress.

Regular corporate meetings are essential for all church members to connect. Meetings make our people to perceive that we are accessible to them. Ephesians 4:16 says, "From whom the whole body, joined and knit together by what every joint supplies, according to the effective working by which every part does its share, causes growth of the body for the edifying of itself in love." Ultimately, the church will grow up into Christ in all aspects, each part fitting together and supporting the other.

Each member of the body must function properly if the body is to grow. Psalm 133:1-3 states, "Behold, how good and how pleasant it is for brethren to dwell together in unity! It is like the precious oil upon the head, running down on the beard, the beard of Aaron, running down on the edge of his garments. It is like the dew of Hermon, descending upon the mountains of Zion; For there the Lord commanded the blessing—Life forevermore."

The people of God are divinely blessed when they walk in unity and operate their spiritual gifts for the edification of the church. Hallelujah! The Psalmist holds up unity as an ideal. Unity in a society is compared to the extravagant blessing of the anointing oil (Psalms 23:5; 36:8; 89:20; and 92:10) or dewfall on dry ground (Genesis 27:28; Proverbs 19:12). Zion was the epitome of blessing because, there, God instituted eternal life - possibly alluding to what Christ accomplished in Jerusalem.

You can only motivate people that can reach you and those that you can reach. Christ, in John 14:16-17, states, "And I will pray the Father, and He will give you another Helper, that He may abide with you forever— the Spirit of truth, whom the world cannot receive, because it neither sees Him nor knows Him; but you know Him, for He dwells with you and will be in you."

"Another Helper" and "the Spirit of truth" refer the Holy Spirit (John 14:26), who guides disciples into all truth (John 16:13). The Spirit replaces Jesus' physical presence by permanently indwelling His followers. Divine presence for Jesus' followers includes the Spirit (John 14:15-17), Jesus (John 14:18-21), and the Father (John 14:22-24). Again, Jesus, in John 16:12-14 says, "I still have many things to say to you, but you cannot bear them now. However, when He, the Spirit of truth, has come, He will guide you into all truth; for He will not speak on His own authority, but whatever He hears He will speak; and He will tell you things to come. He will glorify Me, for He will take of what is Mine and declare it to you."

The Spirit's ministry of guiding Jesus' followers into all truth will fulfill the Psalmist's longing for divine guidance (Psalms 25:4-5; 43:3; 86:11; 143:10). Ken Blanchard and Spence Johnson in the book, "The One Minute Manager", state that the number one motivation of people is "feedback on results." In this regard, church meetings provide a forum for appropriate feedback, while feedbacks ensure that we can do proper monitoring and evaluation of our goals. This facilitates a continuous improvement quality control (QC) such that we can recognize what is working and what is not working and make necessary adjustments. New ideas, initiatives and possibilities are also explored through this quality monitoring process.

2. Operate in the corporate anointing.

No single person can do the work of ministry alone. It has to be a combined effort of believers in harmony. Ephesians 4:11-14 states, "And He Himself gave some to be apostles, some prophets, some evangelists, and some pastors and teachers, for the equipping of the saints for the work of ministry, for the edifying of the body of Christ, till we all come to the unity of the faith and of the knowledge of the Son of God, to a perfect man, to the measure of the stature of the fullness of Christ; that we should no longer be children, tossed to and fro and carried about with every wind of doctrine, by the trickery of men, in the cunning craftiness of deceitful plotting."

Five groups of people gifted by the Spirit of God in the church include: **Apostles** - who are primarily people sent with a divine mission or task. They also serve as spokesmen for God, bringing new revelation and understanding to the church. **Prophets** – who reveal God's will to believers for the present (forthtelling) and predict the future (foretelling). These two are foundational for the church's work (Ephesians 3:5); and in addition to evangelists, they are gifted to spread and plant churches. **Evangelists** proclaim the good news in word and deed and instruct others in evangelism. **Pastors** and teachers shared similar responsibilities. Pastors provide oversight, comfort, and guidance as the church's shepherds (Acts 20:28; 1 Peter 5:1-4). **Teachers** instruct and help to apply God's revelation to the life of the church.

Teachers are concerned with passing on the church's revealed teachings and doctrines (1 Corinthians 15:3-4) rather than bringing new inspirational insights like the prophets. Teachers are indispensable for building up the church and are necessary to enable believers to distinguish false doctrines from the truths of God's word.

The purpose of gifted people is to equip others to minister. When gifted people equip the church, the community of faith will experience stability in precept and practice. Ministry is intended to move believers toward these goals. Maturity (being perfect) and unity are measured in terms of the relationship of the body to the Head, Christ.

Jesus Christ called people to join and help Him fulfill His call. Mark 1:17 says, "Then Jesus said to them, "Follow Me, and I will make you become fishers of men."" Mark includes two accounts of Jesus calling fishermen, two pairs of brothers, to become His disciples. These four form the core of His disciples (Mark 1:29; 3:16-18; 13:3).

It is beneficial to use the win-win approach to motivate church members, since they are mostly volunteers who are not paid any wages for their services to the church. Motivation embraces a win-win concept that provides benefits for all involved in serving. 1 Corinthians 12:7-10 says, "But the manifestation of the Spirit is given to each one for the profit of all: for to one is given the word of wisdom through the Spirit, to another the word of knowledge through the same Spirit, to another faith by the same Spirit, to another gifts of healings by the same Spirit, to another the working of miracles, to another prophecy, to another discerning of spirits, to another different kinds of tongues, to another the interpretation of tongues."

God brings a variety of gifts and manifests diverse ministries and activities within the unified corporate body. These reflect the essential unity and unified work of the persons of the Godhead – the same Spirit, the same Lord, the same God. "Manifestation of the Spirit" refers to gifts, ministries and activities made possible by the Spirit's enabling power. Each is given by God for the mutual benefit of the whole body of believers. The Spirit works supernaturally through a diversity of gifted people to produce one cohesive relationship, and to the profit of all believers.

People should not be manipulated, as this is inappropriate (2 Corinthians 4:2). Manipulation generally benefits one party, while motivation recognizes that we all benefit from the initiative. Manipulation is primarily for the benefit of the "vision proposer", while motivation recognizes the overall contribution of everyone for the benefit of all participants.

Romans 1:11-12 states, "For I long to see you, that I may impart to you some spiritual gift, so that you may be established— that is, that I may be encouraged together with you by the mutual faith both of you and me." Note that the "spiritual gift" mentioned here is not one of the special gifts given by God (1 Corinthians 12:11), but the gifts that Christians gave to one another.

Paul knew that the Roman Christians would minister to him since every part of the body of Christ has useful functions in relation to other parts (1 Corinthians 12:12-27). It is also important to combine collaboration with cooperation in the process of participation. Collaboration involves every sector, recognizing it as being important and a beneficiary, while cooperation primarily benefits one sector. Collaboration encourages and has mutual respect for all sectors and people; builds a positive community spirit; and disapproves of pride and egotism. Romans 12:3-5 says, "For I say, through the grace given to me, to everyone who is among you, not to think of himself more highly than he ought to think, but to think soberly, as God has dealt to each one a measure of faith. For as we have many members in one body, but all the members do not have the same function, so we, being many, are one body in Christ, and individually members of one another."

As part of a renewed mind, the Christian is to think wisely about himself and what function he is to perform in the body of Christ (the church, 1 Corinthians 12:12-28). "Measure of faith" implies that a person should measure himself by the gospel, or by the specific apportionment of faith given to him. Christians are given gifts to use for the good of others (Romans 12:3; 1 Corinthians 12:8-10; Ephesians 4:11; 1 Peter 4:10); therefore, Paul exhorts believers to be humble and to use what God has given them for the good of the body.

Collaboration encompasses corporate responsibility with benefits, while cooperation encourages corporate responsibility without corporate benefits. Hence, a win-win approach remains the best approach since church workers are volunteers. Everyone in the body of Christ is important; there are no useless members and no member can hold the whole body to ransom (Ephesians 4:16).

3. Set well-defined goals.

Endeavor to set goals that will challenge members of the church to have something to anticipate and work towards. This helps to maintain order, avoid pains and frustrations, and ultimately facilitates effective planning. The importance of setting well-defined goals is highlighted in Acts 1:8; Mark 16:15-20; and Matthew 28:18-20 respectively.

Mark 16:15-18 states, "And He said to them, "Go into

all the world and preach the gospel to every creature. He who believes and is baptized will be saved; but he who does not believe will be condemned. And these signs will follow those who believe: In My name they will cast out demons; they will speak with new tongues; they will take up serpents; and if they drink anything deadly, it will by no means hurt them; they will lay hands on the sick, and they will recover."

These verses contain the Great Commission (see also Matthew 28:19; Luke 24:47). To "preach" is imperative, and it is a common binding responsibility. "All the world" refers to the universal and all-inclusive nature of the commission. The elements "believe", and "baptism" were closely related in apostolic preaching (Acts 2:38; 8:36-38; 16:30-33). Jesus named five signs that would accompany not just those who preach, but those who believe. The fact that "In my name" stands out emphatically before any of the enumerated signs emphasizes that the power to do these wonders comes from the risen Lord Himself.

Your goals for the church members must be doable, realistic, measurable and result-oriented. What makes your goals doable is when you fashion them in such a way that they resonate with you and the folks in your team. Measurability often involves setting parameters by which goal accomplishment can be observed, assessed and recorded; it can also involve attaching a numerical value specifically to each goal so that it is in measurable quantities. Jesus, for example, instructed Peter to take the coin from the mouth of the first fish. He also made the disciples to sit the multitudes, who had been listening to Him, in specific groups of 50s before multiplying food.

For your goals to be achievable, they must be actionable (assignable) in order to be attained by participants. It is of vital importance here to remember that we universally operate in the power of God (Philippians 4:13; Zechariah 4:6-7; Ephesians 3:20). Zechariah 4:6-7 states, "This is the word of the Lord to Zerubbabel: Not by might nor by power, but by My Spirit, says the LORD of hosts. Who are you, O great Mountain? Before Zerubbabel you shall become a plain! And he shall bring forth the capstone with shouts of "Grace, grace to it!"

While Zerubbabel was a legitimate heir to David's throne, his role was apparently limited to governor, even though he is spoken of in elevated terms (Haggai 2:21-23). He would be able to move mountains (in hyperbolic language). However, God in His Sovereignty deserves all the credit, while shouts of "grace, grace to the temple" were very appropriate. God's intent is to negate any human claim to might or power, though He empowers human instruments.

Goals must be time-bound, and we need to bring an appropriate time frame to our goals since we will not be here forever. Some goals may be based on short-term planning, while others are long-term. We need to formulate a progressive dimension to accomplishing our goals. A good example is found in Acts 1:8, which we read earlier: "But you shall receive power when the Holy Spirit has come upon you; and you shall be witnesses to Me in Jerusalem, and in all Judea and Samaria, and to the end of the earth."

We must be specific, avoid ambiguity and assumptions in the process of setting our goals to be successful. Hebrews 6:1-3 states, "Therefore, leaving the discussion of the elementary principles of Christ, let us go on to perfection, not laying again the foundation of repentance from dead works and of faith toward God, of the doctrine of baptisms, of laying on of hands, of resurrection of the dead, and of eternal judgment. And this we will do if God permits."

Because of the perils of not progressing, believers are here encouraged to press on toward maturity. Six basic principles are listed as constituting elementary message about the Messiah and serve as the foundation of the Christian faith and life. Categorized into three groups, these principles include: Repentance from sinful actions and faith in God (Hebrews 6:1) - the two sides of conversion that begin the Christian life; baptism of new believers who have received the gospel and laying of hands for Christian leaders to proclaim the gospel (Hebrews 6:2), both of which are fundamental components of church life; the good news of resurrection and the warning of eternal judgment (Hebrews 6:2), which are also essential components of the gospel that the church preaches.

4. Understand your members.

As in all other fields of human endeavors that involve relating with people, it is important to, first and foremost, take time to know and understand the peculiarities of your church members to enable you shepherd them wisely. This knowledge must cut across the individual members and families, as well as the various teams, departments and units that make up the church.

Proverbs 27:23 instructs, "Be diligent to know the state of your flocks and attend to your herds." Solomon here instructs his son, the prince, to pay attention to his people, just as a farmer cares for his livestock. Riches are fickle (Proverbs 23:4-5) and a dynasty can end, but flocks and crops (people and land) are a steady source of sustenance if they are well maintained.

In Solomon's day, after hay was harvested, tender and new grass appeared for grazing. Later, grain was harvested, which along with the hay, provided feed for the livestock. Lambs provided wool; female animals were kept for breeding and milk; while some of the male goats were sold for income that could be reinvested. Similarly, everyone in position of leadership is required to be a good steward of all human and material resources at their disposal. Interactive reinvestments may also be employed to activate and establish inbuilt skills and talents.

If you do not despise the days of little beginning, you can go anywhere from where you are and get anything with the grace of God and the human resources you have. The example of Elisha and the widow's oil confirms that little indeed can be mighty when God is involved. 2 Kings 4:1-5 says, "A certain woman of the wives of the sons of the prophets cried out to Elisha, saying, "Your servant my husband is dead, and you know that your servant feared the Lord. And the creditor is coming to take my two sons to be his slaves." So Elisha said to her, "What shall I do for you? Tell me, what do you have in the house?" And she said, "Your maidservant has nothing in the house but a jar of oil." Then he said, "Go, borrow vessels from everywhere, from all your neighbors—empty vessels; do not gather just a few. And when you have come in, you shall shut the door behind you and your sons; then pour it into all those vessels, and set aside the full ones." So she went from him and shut the door behind her and her sons, who brought the vessels to her; and she poured it out."

The miraculous provision by the man of God, Elisha, for the woman and her children was a private act, but it serves as a public witness to God's miraculous provision. Yes, you can start form where you are, but you must never be limited to where you are or what you have (John 17:20-23). You need to appreciate what you have because what you have is good enough for you to start, since you can only start from where you are, anyway (1 Samuel 22:1; Philemon 1:6). So, know that, for a start, you can only use the people you have, not those you had, desire to have, or even imagine you have (2 Timothy 2:1; Acts 6:3; Genesis 13:13).

Proper placement of church members will facilitate commitment and passion for church service (John 4:34). Such placement cannot be done without knowledge. Adequate knowledge and understanding of your members is paramount to matching their interests to the relevant positions, thus achieving a proper fit - with no square pegs trying to fit into round holes (Ephesians 4:16).

The following are a few of the various areas of ability, which could guide the choice of sections in which to place church members:

- Natural talents – Exodus 31: 1-6

- Spiritual gifts – 1 Corinthians 12:4-11; 18,27

- Business skills – Matthew 4:18-22

- Educational capabilities – Philippians 3:1; Acts 4:13; 18:18; Colossians 4:14

- Secular positions/politics – Luke 5:27-29; 19:1; 23:50

5. Mentor the people.

Apostle Paul charges Timothy in 2 Timothy 1:6-7, "Therefore I remind you to stir up the gift of God which is in you through the laying on of my hands. For God has not given us a spirit of fear, but of power and of love and of a sound mind."

This call to "stir up" does not mean that Timothy had let the fire of the Spirit go out; rather, it was a call to action, lest sluggishness set in. Again, in 2 Timothy 2:1, Paul says to Timothy, "You therefore, my son, be strong in the grace that is in Christ Jesus." The apostle's exhortation here is a continuation of the call to Spirit-empowered boldness earlier stated in 1 Timothy 1:6.

Mentoring provides church members a guided path to excellence, to activate efficiency and effectiveness. Moreover, a major reason for mentoring people is to enable them to project a corporate image of the church, which essentially constitutes the main vision and identity of the ministry. Part of this is usually reflected in the name and divine emphasis of the ministry.

The name of my church, for example, is Living Word Chapel (LWC), where the word is working wonders. The corporate name of our bigger international ministry is the Redeemed Christian Church of God (RCCG), which brands our corporate image on redemption. Our other denominational parishes adopt various significant names, such as Restoration Chapel, Grace Assembly, Dominion Chapel, Isaac Generation, Jesus House and so on - to define and brand their respective corporate images.

The three key stages of mentoring include:

- **Mandating or commissioning members** (Mark 16:15; Matthew 28:18). This is the end-point of the empowering process that makes the people feel trusted and consequently building their confidence. It frees the action teams from micro-managing. Essentially, this process is a way of telling members, "You make your decisions; do it while I am not there and report back to me later."

- **Role-modeling.** This is about being a good example, because people tend to do what they see, not necessarily what they are told. It is far more effective when the teacher presents himself as an exemplary model to the people, rather than just brandishing a motto.

- **Monitoring.** Since people often do what you inspect, not just what you expect, monitoring guarantees appropriate inspection. This process also ensures that they are doing things right, alongside doing the right things.

6. Train and equip people.

Regular training sessions are required to build competence, which reinforces confidence. This is another essential aspect of the mentoring process. Appropriate tools must be supplied to people to accomplish what they ought to do (Mark 1:17; Acts 18:18). Availability of proper training and tools encourage people to work, since it makes the work easier and more enjoyable.

Apostle Paul exhorted the Ephesian elders, mentoring them through training and equipping with appropriate spiritual and physical tools. Acts 20:20 says, "How I kept back nothing that was helpful, but proclaimed it to you, and taught you publicly and from house to house."

The mark of a truly faithful teacher of the gospel is to keep back nothing that, though unpopular or personally difficult, is helpful for the disciples. Acts 20:28 also states, "Therefore take heed to yourselves and to all the flock, among which the Holy Spirit has made you overseers, to shepherd the church of God which He purchased with His own blood."

7. Pray for them.

1 Timothy 2:1-4 instructs, "Therefore I exhort first of all that supplications, prayers, intercessions, and giving of thanks be made for all men, for kings and all who are in authority, that we may lead a quiet and peaceable life in all godliness and reverence. For this is good and acceptable in the sight of God our Savior, who desires all men to be saved and to come to the knowledge of the truth."

The most important key to motivating our people is praying consistently for them. We must pray passionately and persistently (Luke 18:1; 1 Thessalonians 5:17). Motivation goes beyond the physical realm and requires clear spiritual control and influences (Zechariah 4:6-7; Matthew 11:28-30). This was what Jesus did, and is still doing (Romans 8:34; Hebrews 7:25). Jesus said that He would be the one to build His church, and that He would make us fishers of men (Matthew 16:16-19).

We can emulate the pattern of the Apostle Paul in what has come to be known as the "Pauline prayers" (Colossians 1:3; 4:12-13; 1 Thessalonians 1:2-3;

2 Thessalonians 1:3; 2 Timothy 1:3; Romans 1:8; Ephesians 1:16; 3:14; Philippians 1:3). He often prayed for the people under his care and also ensured that his companions were equally mentored to be intercessors.

8. Recognize and praise accomplishments.

Ephesians 1:15-18 states, "Therefore I also, after I heard of your faith in the Lord Jesus and your love for all the saints, do not cease to give thanks for you, making mention of you in my prayers: that the God of our Lord Jesus Christ, the Father of glory, may give to you the spirit of wisdom and revelation in the knowledge of Him, the eyes of your understanding being enlightened; that you may know what is the hope of His calling, what are the riches of the glory of His inheritance in the saints."

Paul wrote and sent letters to the Ephesians, the Colossians, and Philemon at the same time he received word about the faith and love of the believers in Asia Minor. For the Ephesian believers, in particular, he wanted them to understand what great spiritual resources were theirs in Christ. "Revelation" refers to the insight and discernment that the Spirit brings to the mysteries of divine truth. Paul wanted them to have a spirit of wisdom so that they might get to know God more completely. He prayed for the church not only to understand but to experience these blessings.

It is pertinent to remember that church members are mostly volunteers, and we must praise and thank them (privately and publicly) for the things they do. You may need to identify and get influencers in the church to help you. They may or may not be people in key positions in the church. These are the ones that when they speak, everyone listens. Share your visions with them and see if they may be a positive influence on the more rigid members.

Everyone naturally loves compliments; it drives people to perform better. Apostle Paul took time to always appreciate the people he worked with, and this provided positive reinforcement.

You can organize periodic social get-togethers to celebrate your members and award prizes during such special occasions. Get-togethers and social interactions help to build friendship, community spirit, and a worker-friendly atmosphere.

Christians must believe in the power of supernatural motivation. Psalm 110:3 says, "Your people shall be volunteers in the day of your power; in the beauties of holiness, from the womb of the morning, y o u have the dew of your youth." God says that His people will be willing in the day of His power – and this should make us believe in the power of supernatural motivation. Interestingly, the above verse is often tagged the most obscure in the book of Psalms. "Volunteers" is the same word used for freewill offerings; so the people of God offer themselves for service, beautiful in their armor, and holy in their attitude. "From the womb of the morning" depicts the people's eagerness to do battle for Yahweh and His Messiah. Hallelujah!

Chapter 3

SMALL GROUPS: PURPOSE AND PATTERN

"Small numbers make no difference to God. There is nothing small if God is in it." - D.L. MOODY

Though it may not be so apparent, the fact is that more and more people today are searching for purpose and meaning in life. Certainly, the battle against darkness is not decreasing. In fact, statistics reveal that only four percent of today's youths will embrace evangelical Christianity, while they devote their lives to the vanities of life. This new trend offers abundant opportunities for Christians to reach out with the supernatural power of God to influence their culture.

Jesus, in Luke 10:2-3, rouses us to the vastness of

ripened harvests all around us. At the same time, He reminds us that the harvesters are few and thus challenges us to take urgent steps to salvage the situation. He says, "The harvest truly is great, but the laborers are few; therefore pray the Lord of the harvest to send out laborers into His harvest. Go your way; behold, I send you out as lambs among wolves."

Christ seems to be saying that, as great as the spiritual harvest was, the seventy whom He sent out to preach were not enough. There was need for many more to take the message, and prayers must be offered to meet this need. Ironically, what many of us do in our comfortable churches is to sit back and wait for the lost to stroll in; and while we do, multitudes of souls continue to perish out there. The challenge for us is that we have to bring in the harvest, and thereafter ensure that we disciple and keep them in the Lord.

BIBLICAL FOUNDATION FOR SMALL GROUPS

One effective way of bringing in the harvest of souls is revealed in the Old Testament by Jethro, the father-in-law of Moses. Moses was significantly limited in his administrative impact as he tried to singlehandedly oversee the Israelites from morning till late night every day. Unsurprisingly, he could not meet all the needs of the people, even as he almost wore himself out. As God would have it, it was at this time that Jethro paid him a visit and gave him the following life-saving and ministry-boosting piece of advice:

"Both you and these people who are with you will surely wear yourselves out. For this thing is too much for you; you are not able to perform it by yourself. Listen now to my voice; I will give you counsel, and God will be with you: Stand before God for the people, so that you may bring the difficulties to God. And you shall teach them the statutes and the laws, and show them the way in which they must walk and the work they must do. Moreover you shall select from all the people able men, such as fear God, men of truth, hating covetousness; and place such over them to be rulers of thousands, rulers of hundreds, rulers of fifties, and rulers of tens. And let them judge the people at all times. Then it will be that every great matter they shall bring to you, but every small matter they themselves shall judge. So it will be easier for you, for they will bear the burden with you" (Exodus 18:18-22).

It is in the above passage that we have the first mention of small groups in the Scripture. Without breaking the church into manageable small groups, some folks may be totally left out of the body. Thus, small groups constitute the divine key for reaping the harvests promptly, as well as for maximizing the potentials of every believer within the body of Christ.

The operation and potentials of the small group are also demonstrated in the growth of the early church. We find a good example in Acts 6:1-4, which states: "Now in those days, when the number of the disciples was multiplying, there arose a complaint against the Hebrews by the Hellenists, because their widows were neglected in the daily distribution. Then the twelve summoned the multitude of the disciples and said, "It is not desirable that we should leave the word of God and serve tables. Therefore, brethren, seek out from among you seven men of good reputation, full of the Holy Spirit and wisdom, whom we may appoint over this business; but we will give ourselves continually to prayer and to the ministry of the word."

The Hellenists (Greek-speaking Jews) complained against the (native) Hebrews, because their widows were being overlooked in the daily serving of food. When church population increases remarkably, natural effectiveness dwindles, culminating in offensive issues like the oversight in the above passage. Without small life-support groups, inefficiency will eventually lead to conflicts among brethren, which is unhealthy for the body of Christ. This is why we must take the place of small groups very seriously in our churches. Small groups have tremendous and unlimited benefits. They are like the cells in our body - the healthier they are, the healthier our body will be. They have the power and potential to radically change lives through mutual prayers and practical love demonstrated within the group. They, consequently, in the process of time, become centers where miracles frequently happen, to the glory of God and edification of the saints.

NECESSITY OF SMALL GROUPS

Psychologists have revealed that people have a fundamental need for inclusion in group life and for close relationships. This confirms that human beings are not created to be alone. We naturally need friendship and fellowship, just as we need food, to survive. Most importantly, the desire of God is that all His children connect and relate often with one another (1 Peter 4:7-9; Hebrews 10:25; Ecclesiastes 4:9; Genesis 2:18; 1 Thessalonians 5:14).

Relationships happen only when we reach out; as such, we have to be intentional in developing one another spiritually, physically, and materially. We are commissioned to reach out together. 1 Peter 4:7-9 states, "But the end of all things is at hand; therefore be serious and watchful in your prayers. And above all things have fervent love for one another, for "love will cover a multitude of sins." Be hospitable to one another without grumbling."

Peter exhorts believers to maintain unity, while doing everything to God's glory. "Love will cover a multitude of sins" means that love repeatedly forgives (Proverbs 10:12). Believers must not strive or complain at other believers, even when under persecution; rather, we must be hospitable at all times.

Concerning the value of friendship and companionship, Ecclesiastes 4:9-10 states, "Two are better than one, Because they have a good reward for their labor. For if they fall, one will lift up his companion. But woe to him who is alone when he falls, for he has no one to help him up."

Quite instructively, friendship is one area of life that the "Preacher" in Ecclesiastes never calls "vanity". In view of this, small groups should be organized around affinity or collective interests. They can be based on age groups – for example, children, youths, young adults, elders, and so on. They can also be tied to neighborhoods, zip codes and counties, as well as other common interests. Examples could be business clubs, sports groups, new settlers in USA, miracle mothers (comprising expectant mothers and those seeking the fruit of the womb), singles, missions, and so forth.

HOW THE SMALL GROUP WORKS

Members of small groups live and experience life together in a state of mutual fellowship, thereby growing deeper and progressive in their walk with the Lord. They increase in number through evangelism and reaching out to others, resulting in fervent church growth. Acts 2:47 says, "…And the Lord added to the church daily those who were being saved."

The entire body and fellowship edify and minister to one another reverently (1 Corinthians 12:14-27). To foster this, accountability should be maintained by each member of the group. Every member encourages and greatly urges their brothers and sisters to better follow the Lord (Matthew 18:15-20). Galatians 6:1-5 says, "Brethren, if a man is overtaken in any trespass, you who are spiritual restore such a one in a spirit of gentleness, considering yourself lest you also be tempted. Bear one another's burdens, and so fulfill the law of Christ. For if anyone thinks himself to be something, when he is nothing, he deceives himself. But let each one examine his own work, and then he will have rejoicing in himself alone, and not in another. For each one shall bear his own load."

A person who falls into sin at a vulnerable point should be spiritually restored with gentleness (a part of the fruit of the Spirit – Galatians 5:23). However, those doing such restoration should themselves be careful to avoid being pulled into the sin. A believer whose life is controlled by the Holy Spirit manifests this by coming alongside to help bear the emotional, physical or spiritual burden threatening to crush his fellow believer. The law of Christ is "love one another, as I have loved you" (John 13:34).

The good news is that though it was not possible to keep the entire law of Moses (Galatians 3:10, 12), now it is possible to fulfill both that law (Galatians 5:14) and the law of Christ through loving actions. No one should consider himself superior to a fallen believer; otherwise, such a person would be deceiving himself and unknowingly exposing himself to temptation and defeat also. It is illegitimate to compare ourselves to another, because the Lord assigns each person a different load and capacity to fulfill His purpose for our lives.

Believers are divinely commissioned to reach out together. Using the small life-support groups facilitates an efficient means of implementing a major command to reach outside the church's walls to bring people to Christ. Philippians 1:27-28 states, "Only let your conduct be worthy of the gospel of Christ, so that whether I come and see you or am absent, I may hear of your affairs, that you stand fast in one spirit, with one mind striving together for the faith of the gospel, and not in any way terrified by your adversaries, which is to them a proof of perdition, but to you of salvation, and that from God."

Paul here reminds the church of its higher citizenship in the Kingdom of God. He exhorts that the church must manifest the same readiness demonstrated by the Roman armies as they regularly stood ready for combat, regardless of the enemy's level of strength and preparedness, or even the distracting enticements of culture. "One spirit" underscores the believer's unified attitude, while "one mind" ("same soul") implies that believers share "life" in all ramifications.

Paul urged believers to bond together in love and prevent divisiveness. Standing firm and working together in harmony, not individualism, achieves God's purposes. The fact remains that "we" is always more powerful than "me". Partnership is powerful, especially when we are working together in groups to tell the world about Jesus.

Evangelism naturally involves team effort, even in those times we think we are working alone. The reality is that before we eventually bring someone to Christ, the Holy Spirit must have been at work in that life, while other believers must have also been influential, directly or indirectly. This is why Paul, in 1 Corinthians 3:6-7, says, "I planted, Apollos watered, but God gave the increase. So then neither he who plants is anything, nor he who waters, but God who gives the increase."

Paul enlightened the Corinthian believers that both

The Living Church

he and Apollos, the founding evangelists of the Corinthian church, were dispatched ministers through whom they (the Corinthians) had believed the message of the gospel. "Planted" is regarded as a reference to Paul's founding of the church, while "watered" refers to Apollo's later ministry after Paul had left Corinth. Ultimately, the Lord was to receive all the credit for the growth; therefore, the servants were nothing but mere messengers.

No minister ever needs to flag his own reputation at the expense of God's glory. Paul and Apollos were equal servants in the gospel work, and each would receive commendation for his labor among the Corinthian believers (God's field) when the Lord returned (1 Corinthians 4:4-5). We are to work together as partners who belong to God, and because two can accomplish more than twice as much as one (Ecclesiastes 4:9).

Paul, again, tells the Corinthian believers, "For we are God's fellow workers; you are God's field, you are God's building. According to the grace of God which was given to me, as a wise master builder I have laid the foundation, and another builds on it. But let each one take heed how he builds on it" (1 Corinthians 3:9-10).

The value of small groups is paramount in allowing believers to work side by side towards leading our friends and family members to Christ. We can draw strength and encouragement from one another as we bring our personal friends into His presence. We find a biblical example in the case of the four friends who brought their paralyzed friend to Jesus by breaking through the roof in a crowded room, and the friend receive his healing (Mark. 2:1-12).

BIBLICAL PATTERN FOR SMALL GROUPS

The Bible pattern is God's pattern. Believers sometimes prefer to do certain things their own way, since God's system sometimes does not function the way they expect. In view of this, different folks have used different methods, some of which some have worked well, while others have not - leading to instability.

However, the guarantee is that God's system always proves to be the best in the end. Small groups exist for the purpose of fellowship, prayer, spiritual growth, mutual support and so on (Matthew 18:19-20). They enable friendship to develop by rendering support and encouragement. The Bible pattern of such groups emerged when Moses' father-in-law advised him (as we read earlier). Moses consequently appointed rulers of 10, 50, 100, and 1,000 people, as his representatives, in lieu of his sole (personal) management of the crowd.

In the New Testament, Acts 2:46-47 says, "So continuing daily with one accord in the temple, and breaking bread from house to house, they ate their food with gladness and simplicity of heart, praising God and having favor with all the people. And the Lord added to the church daily those who were being saved."

Early Christian gatherings took place in two places - the temple and the homes of believers - while a vital church grew through the unction of the Holy Spirit. Hallelujah! The church was an evangelizing church, growing steadily and daily. The gift of evangelism took place primarily through the gathering of Christians in the temple and in homes. The crucifixion and resurrection of Christ were at the heart of their preaching, and this called for immediate response from anyone who listened.

We can learn a lot from these scriptural approaches to small groups, so that each group in our local churches becomes a dominant force in populating and advancing the corporate body and the Kingdom of God, in general.

PRAYER AND EVANGELISM IN THE SMALL GROUP

God intends for us to work together, side by side, in a group, to experience the privilege and joy of helping someone come to Christ. Grasping the fact that you can help bring other people to Christ as part of a group effort usually causes a marvelous turnaround in the life of a believer.

The first step in the small group, prior to evangelism, is to pray together before we start to witness. The primary reason is that we cannot pray for people and not become concerned about them. Moreover, there are certain ways the small group can pray for nonbelieving friends and family members. We can, for example, pray for an opportunity to talk to them about Jesus and to invite them to church.

Don't give room to unbelief because God will surely answer that fervent prayer! Colossians 4:2-4 states, "Continue earnestly in prayer, being vigilant in it with thanksgiving; meanwhile praying also for us, that God would open to us a door for the word, to speak the mystery of Christ, for which I am also in chains, that I may make it manifest, as I ought to speak."

The second step is to pray for God to soften the heart of the people, since God usually softens the hearts of those He is trying to reach by sending the rain in advance. You can, for example, discern that God is softening a person's heart when they are going through the storms of life.

Third, pray for God to fill your heart with genuine concern and compassion for others. Perhaps, you are currently insensitive to the plights of the lost and the hurting around you. You cannot be effective in soul-winning with such a heart. You need to pray that God will soften your heart. As you do, God will soon fill your heart with a "burden", which expresses that your heart is now tender towards other people. This is a new height and another level of spiritual maturity in the life of a believer, as his priority will henceforth be to pray for other people.

Fourth, pray that the words of Christ will emerge from within you and cause a groundswell of positive response from the people, similar to what happened among the early Christians. 2 Thessalonians 3:1-3 states, "Finally, brethren, pray for us, that the word of the Lord may run swiftly and be glorified, just as it is with you, and that we may be delivered from unreasonable and wicked men; for not all have faith. But the Lord is faithful, who will establish you and guard you from the evil one." Paul here reminds us that the Lord is faithful, despite the activities of the evil one and his agents.

In addition to all these prayers, the leadership of the group must take strategic actions and be inventive in the way the group invites those being prayed for in the group setting. Other unconventional ways of approach may include having a barbecue, a movie night, a game night, a dessert night and so on. Colossians 4:5-6 says, "Walk in wisdom toward those who are outside, redeeming the time. Let your speech always be with grace, seasoned with salt, that you may know how you ought to answer each one."

Paul exhorts us here to apply wisdom in our interaction with unbelievers (see also Colossians 1:9-10). The word "redeeming" comes from a verb meaning "to buy up", as if finding a bargain. It apparently conveys the idea of making the most of our time spent with unbelievers.

A PRAYER MODEL FOR SMALL GROUPS

As we wrap up this portion of our discussion on small groups, here is a model prayer that encompasses the key points we should be emphasizing in our respective prayer groups:

> *"Glorious Father, we bless your holy name and ask you to use our group to "reach one more for Jesus". Fill us with a deep concern for people who don't know Jesus, and prompt us to pray consistently and persistently for their salvation.*
>
> *"We appreciate that you paid a high price to bring all of us into the family, and we agree with you that no one is hopeless or beyond the reach of your love. Guide us as we reach out in your name and give us inventive creativity to our methods for outreach.*

The Living Church

"Our Eternal Rock of Ages, we ask in faith that our small group will continue to succeed in winning souls for you. We lift this prayer in the name of Jesus. Amen".

The Lord will surely reward our labors and prayers with extraordinary results!

CHAPTER 4

SMALL GROUPS: IMPACTS AND LEADERSHIP

"It takes more than a busy church, a friendly church, or even an evangelical church to impact a community for Christ. It must be a church ablaze, led by leaders who are ablaze for God." - WESLEY L. DUEWEL

After over two decades of relentless outreach among the people of the New Hebrides islands (now known as Vanuatu), a memorial tablet was erected in honor of Dr. John Geddie, Scots-Canadian missionary who, together with his small missionary team, had labored so hard among the people. On the tablet was this inscription:

"When he landed, in 1848, there were no Christians. When he left, in 1872, there were no heathen."

This is a great testimony to the power and influence that committed believers can wield in their communities and beyond, regardless of their number. As already emphasized in the previous chapter, organizing the church into small groups of people, all working together for the glory of God and growth of the body is of utmost importance. In the same way that Dr. Geddie and his small evangelical group mightily influenced the Hebrides islands for Christ and transformed the lives of the people, so also do small groups of consecrated believers within the church have the potential to spark and sustain revival within the church and the entire community.

Let's explore the power of the small group in detail.

IMPACTS OF THE SMALL GROUP

1. Small groups grow the church spiritually.

The book of Acts shows how the early church grew spiritually. Acts 2:1-4 narrates, "When the Day of Pentecost had fully come, they were all with one accord in one place. And suddenly there came a sound from heaven, as of a rushing mighty wind, and it filled the whole house where they were sitting. Then there appeared to them divided tongues, as of fire, and one sat upon each of them. And they were all filled with the Holy Spirit and began to speak with other tongues, as the Spirit gave them utterance."

The events of Pentecost, which mark the formal and public beginning of the church, involved a number of supernatural phenomena. These included the rush of a violent wind from heaven, tongues like flames of fire, the infilling with the Holy Spirit, and speaking in languages as the Spirit gave believers the ability to function. These languages that the Spirit empowered the believers to speak have been interpreted as: (1) supernatural languages given specifically for the purpose of communicating with the people gathered from all over the Roman Empire; (2) human languages that were recognized by individuals from various lands; or (3) the Greek language that was common to all the people gathered throughout the Roman world.

Other characteristics of that remarkable day of Pentecost and thereafter that will prove highly beneficial to our groups included:

- The believers were joined together in unity of purpose – Acts 1:14.

- They were filled with the Holy Spirit – Acts 2:1-4.

- The new converts continued in the apostles' doctrines – Acts 2:42.

- The word spread throughout the entire region – Acts 12:24.

The Living Church

- The disciples were filled with the Holy Spirit – Acts 13:52.

- The church was strengthened in the faith – Acts 16:5.

- The members searched the scriptures every day – Acts 17:11.

- The word spread widely and grew in power – Acts 19:20.

As members of the early church gathered in small groups wherever and whenever they could, miracles that glorified Christ happened severally, and God's power through faith was at work. There were extraordinary healings, such that even Peter's shadow made people whole, which demonstrated his identity as an apostle (Acts 5:15-16). A similar thing happened with Paul: "Now God worked unusual miracles by the hands of Paul, so that even handkerchiefs or aprons were brought from his body to the sick, and the diseases left them and the evil spirits went out of them" (Acts 19:11-12).

Acts 19:13-17 further reveals that certain itinerant Jewish exorcists attempted to use Jesus' name to command evil spirits. This actually involved ancient magic traditions by the invocation of divine names. However, the name of the Lord Jesus, rather than being abused, was magnified when people realized the power of the Lord was not available for just anyone to manipulate.

2. Small groups increase the church numerically.

The book of Acts also shows us how the early church grew numerically. Acts 1:15 says, "And in those days Peter stood up in the midst of the disciples (altogether the number of names was about a hundred and twenty)…" In the very next chapter, however, we are told, "Then those who gladly received his word were baptized; and that day about three thousand souls were added to them. And they continued steadfastly in the apostles' doctrine and fellowship, in the breaking of bread, and in prayers" (Acts 2:41-42).

An estimated 3,000 people became Christians in response to Peter's preaching. There was also a very close link between coming to faith and being baptized, as apparently there was no delay between the two. The large number was a reflection of the huge crowds who had travelled to Jerusalem from all over the Mediterranean region for the Passover celebration.

The four practices in Acts 2:41-42 – learning doctrines, fellowshipping, breaking of bread and praying – provide insights into the priorities of early Christianity. These same practices should be considered normative for the church today, as well as for all the groups within the church. The "apostles' doctrines" was similar to Peter's message at Pentecost which focused on making Christ known by appealing to eyewitness testimony and prophecies of the Old Testament. Early Christians gathered together regularly for edification, prayer and exhortation. The breaking of bread included fellowship meals and participation in the Lord's Supper (1 Corinthians 11:17-34).

When 3,000 people were added according to Acts 2:41, the small group immediately grew into a mega church. In Acts 4:4, 5,000 men were added; and it will, therefore, be correct to say there would have been about 10,000 women and children. A great number were later added (Acts 5:14), while the disciples increased rapidly (Acts 6:1).

Other events that gladdened the early believers include: those living in Lydia's house were baptized (Acts 16:14-15). A great number in Antioch turned to the Lord (Acts 11:21-26); the church in Galatia grew in number daily (Acts 6:5); and many more people believed (Acts 17:4,12).

3. Small groups are epicenters of miracles.

When any small group sets goals and are pursuing their dreams with vigor, God says nothing they aim to do will be withheld from them (Genesis 11:6). The paralyzed man got his miracle because his small group would not accept no for an answer as they burst open the roof of the house to let down their friend to receive his healing miracle from Christ in the midst of a crowd (Mark 2:1-4).

Unusual (supernatural) things happen when small groups operate in the power of the Spirit. Peter and John were arrested but later released and forbidden from using the name of Jesus. However, while the small group of believers prayed after hearing the report, the place where they were began to shake (Acts 4:13-31).

At a time, Herod began to harass the church, and even killed James. However, when he again took Peter, the small group began to pray, and God sent an angel to release Peter from prison; a confirmation that incredible things and miracles happen when small groups pray (Acts 12:1-19).

In the Old Testament, we are told that Elisha visited the small group at Gilgal and asked them to feed everyone despite that there was famine. In the process, a killer poison was discovered in the pot, and death was reversed. Hallelujah! (2 Kings 4:38-41).

I recall when our Pastor at Living Word Chapel, Houston, invited church members in 2018 to start donating their houses to be used for conducting fellowship and worship (as small group centers), where each neighborhood would periodically gather, we were slow to respond. However, the trend changed to a very positive response after series of rigorous sermons and workshops were conducted to further educate the congregation on the spiritual benefits derived thereof from having a small group center in individual family homes. The church members became more informed and understood that every home God uses has been radically transformed as revealed in the case of Obed-Edom. Scripture reveals how the Ark of God was brought to Jerusalem by King David. 2 Samuel 6:11-12 states, "The ark of the Lord remained in the house of Obed-Edom the Gittite three months. And the Lord blessed Obed-Edom and all his household. Now it was told King David, saying, "The Lord has blessed the house of Obed-Edom and all that belongs to him, because of the ark of God." So David went and brought up the ark of God from the house of Obed-Edom to the City of David with gladness."

Considering the blessings that proceed from the small group, we should all be glad and excited to yield our homes for use as a small group center.

YOU AND THE SMALL GROUP

Small groups have tremendous benefits required by Christians to grow in a healthy spiritual and physical environment. Members of the group help and support each other such that no one really lacks anything because they practice the love of Christ by supporting one another (Acts 4:32-37).

For you, in particular, the following are some of the blessings you derive from identifying with a small group in the church:

- Small groups are the place to identify and develop your spiritual gifts.

- Small groups furnish and fortify you with the systems that help you weather life's storms because two are always better than one (Ecclesiastes 4:9-12).

- You really feel at home in a small group, and you are able to really feel and enjoy your sense of belonging to the church body.

- It is in small groups that you can really ask questions, and consequently grow progressively while you get "close up" answers to your questions.

- You get the accountability that you really need in small groups for a healthy spiritual growth.

- Small groups are a safe place to be vulnerable, to open up, to make mistakes, and learn effectively from correct answers for increased wisdom.

- Knowing and fearing God is what small groups strive and labor to achieve. You will drift through life unknowingly if God doesn't direct your path, and the small group is your antidote for aimlessness and godlessness (Acts 13:1-3).

- Dorcas had a small group in her home. When she died, the people rallied and got Peter to raise her back to life (Acts 9:36-43). Indeed, small groups are life extenders.

- It's a terrible and most undesirable thing if you are without the support of a small group in the day of need (Ecclesiastes 4:9-10). There was no one to rescue Abel, because he had no small group (Genesis 4:9). The plight of the paralyzed man was similar as he waited helplessly for 38 years, without anyone to help him (John 5:1-9).

LEADERSHIP OF SMALL GROUPS

John Maxwell, a reputable author on leadership, once stated that "everything rises and falls on leadership." This principle is clearly exemplified throughout the Scripture. Typical examples include King David and his mighty men (2 Samuel 23:8-39); Peter and the disciples (John 21:3-4); and James and the early church (Acts 15:13-22).

Acts 15:13-14 says, "And after they had become silent, James answered, saying, "Men and brethren, listen to me: Simon has declared how God at the first visited the Gentiles to take out of them a people for His name." As the leader of the Jerusalem church, James, the half-brother of Jesus, assessed the claims and counterclaims from members of the early church. He began his address by recalling how Simon (Peter) had reported God's plan to visit the Gentiles, which had occasioned a controversy of its own (Acts 11:2-18). James cited the Prophet Amos (Amos 9:11-12) and Prophet Isaiah (Isaiah 45:21) to demonstrate that God had long ago foretold that the Gentiles would be called by His name. James' position as the first among equals in the Jerusalem church is seen in his passing a "sentence" after the debate.

Therefore, it is pertinent to affirm that the productivity of any small group will be a function of the leader's effectiveness, which reflects in his or her ability to influence and motivate members consistently, and successfully produce the desired results. It is therefore essential that we all imbibe and cultivate the values for effective and fruit-bearing leadership, since God has fortified every believer to bear fruit (John 15:16).

QUALIFICATIONS OF A SMALL GROUP LEADER

An essential and fundamental qualification of a small group leader is that he or she must be born again (John 3:1-21; 2 Corinthians 5:17; 1 Corinthians 2:14). John 3:4-7 states, "Nicodemus said to Him, "How can a man be born when he is old? Can he enter a second time into his mother's womb and be born?" Jesus answered, "Most assuredly, I say to you, unless one is born of water and the Spirit, he cannot enter the kingdom of God. That which is born of the flesh is flesh, and that which is born of the Spirit is spirit. Do not marvel that I said to you, 'You must be born again.'"

The spiritual rebirth informs the reference to the "children of God" – that is, those who are "born" of God. Being "born of water and the Spirit" refers to the spiritual birth that cleanses from sin and brings spiritual transformation (Ezekiel 36:25-27). Jesus illustrated His pronouncement with an analogy of the wind and a person of the Spirit. While their origins are invisible, their effects can be observed.

2 Corinthians 5:17 says, "Therefore, if anyone is in Christ, he is a new creation; old things have passed away; behold, all things have become new.". The words "in Christ" refer to being in union with Him. It is

not about reforming the old nature, but a genuine conversion that begins with life transformation. The indwelling Spirit creates the divine life in believers (Romans 8:8-10), enabling a life of new things. This is also expressed elsewhere in the Scripture as "regeneration" or "born-again" (John 3:3-8; Titus 3:5; 1 Peter 1:23). Being born again implies that those who were enemies of God have become His children by being reconciled to Him.

Moreover, the work of a small leader can only be done in the power of the Holy Spirit. This means that a leader must be baptized with the Holy Spirit, with the evidence of speaking in tongues (Acts 1:8; 19:11-20; Romans 8:14-17). Any believer that is saved and baptized with the Holy Spirit can successfully step in and perform this role. Of course, you will still have to continue to grow progressively, just as the entire fellowship group, towards maturity and perfection.

Romans 8:14-17 says, "For as many as are led by the Spirit of God, these are sons of God. For you did not receive the spirit of bondage again to fear, but you received the Spirit of adoption by whom we cry out, "Abba, Father." The Spirit Himself bears witness with our spirit that we are children of God, and if children, then heirs—heirs of God and joint heirs with Christ, if indeed we suffer with Him, that we may also be glorified together."

The leading of the Spirit of God is His providential sanctification (Psalm 23:3) - which is also common to all sons, and will bring the believer to glory (Romans 8:17). This leading of the Spirit is not mystical; it is the Spirit's empowerment for mortification of fleshly desires.

CORE RESPONSIBILITIES OF A SMALL GROUP LEADER

The small group leader is required to demonstrate exemplary leadership traits, while everyone else in the group assists in unity and team spirit. Our goal, as members of God's Family, is to embrace and involve everyone, and to keep inviting the unsaved, our friends, families, and co-workers. Ultimately, we strive to see that we all grow together, making prayer our core value, loving and caring for one another and growing numerically and spiritually. As we increase in number, we can eventually break into smaller units and reproduce our population within every 4 to 6 months maximum time period.

The responsibilities of the small group leader, therefore, include:

- Making prayer the core value of everything for the group.

- Making spiritual growth and soul-winning outreaches the focus of the group.

- Formulating and communicating (with progressive implementation) the vision of the group.

- Caring for all participants, following up and praying for them.

- Mentoring others by individually involving them in various aspects of the meetings and all activities.

- Building faith and hope in the group.

- Monitoring others and all their activities, and instilling in them the principles of time management.

- Dividing and delegating responsibilities to provide opportunities for everyone to always participate.

- Engaging everyone in leading worship, prayers, offering, questions and answers.

- Encouraging feedbacks and addressing them accordingly; or consulting with the Pastor of the main church ultimately.

SUCCESS STRATEGIES IN LEADING THE SMALL GROUP

1. Embrace the vision and assignment in the place of prayers.

The vision is the ability to project imagination and grasp the concept of the desired future result; while the assignment is to convey your members to that desired end. It is not possible for one to rise beyond the vision in one's heart. However, if a leader has not fully grasped the small group's vision (as communicated by the church leadership), it will be futile to embark on the assignment (Proverb 29:18; Ecclesiastes 10:15).

Proverbs 29:18 states, "Where there is no revelation, the people cast off restraint; But happy is he who keeps the law." "Revelation" refers to the inspired message from God; in this case, the wisdom of proverbs. The happiest are found within God's plan (Proverbs 3:13-18). When we incubate the vision in the place of prayers (and fasting), our hearts will be broadened to see God's perspective on how to actualize the desired future (vision) within our sphere of influence (the assignment) (Job 32:8).

2. Be goal-oriented.

Being very specific on the goals will help the group to focus their efforts on timeframes, as well as inspire intelligence, innovation and creativities. It will also strengthen and challenge their "faith walk" (Proverbs 14:23; James 2:20).

The praying effort will enlighten our minds to articulate the vision clearly in practical actionable goals (Proverbs 24:27; Isaiah 28:10). To facilitate effectiveness, the goals must be clear, attainable and measurable (Luke 14:28-32). For instance, with the goal to invite at least three souls per month, members need to invite one new "un-churched" person to each meet-up etc. The bottom line is that we can only expect increase from God when we diligently "put our feet to our faith" through attainable goals (Proverbs 28:19; Isaiah 2:20).

3. Partner with the Holy Spirit.

Believers are God's workmanship and function as His partners, while God has given us the privilege to partner with Him in achieving His purpose and plans on earth (Ephesians 2:10; 1 Corinthians 3:9). Therefore, it is wise and appropriate that we acknowledge Him (in the person of the Holy Spirit) as our helper if we are to be productive in our assignment.

The Holy Spirit is designated the "Comforter", that is, the One called alongside to help (John 14:16, 26; 15:26; 16:7). He will teach and equip us to profit in every leadership assignment if we consult Him (Isaiah 48:17; 1 John 2:20, 27). Isaiah 48:17 says, "Thus says the Lord, your Redeemer, The Holy One of Israel: "I am the Lord your God, Who teaches you to profit, Who leads you by the way you should go."

Isaiah concluded on Israel's being refined for God's glory by affirming that God was the One who had brought him to the people. Our sufficiency is indeed from God. 2 Corinthians 3:4-5 states, "And we have such trust through Christ toward God. Not that we are sufficient of ourselves to think of anything as being from ourselves, but our sufficiency is from God."

Paul is confident, but not arrogant. There is no sufficiency for the Christian's ministry, except from God.

4. Empower your members.

Members can only achieve productivity in terms of "sustainable membership production", when the leader empowers others to lead (Acts 6:3-4). This is made possible when the incumbent leader essentially sees everyone as a priest (that is, one appointed to serve the master), and willing to create opportunities for them to establish and express their God-given gifting (1 Peter 2:9; Ephesians 2:10). As each part of the body contributes its share, growth is promoted, and new leaders are groomed for future assignments (Ephesians 4:16; 2 Timothy 2:2).

5. **Be a servant-leader.**

Another important virtue that can promote effective leadership is having a servant's heart (Luke 22:27), which encompasses humility, authenticity, integrity and faithfulness (1 Corinthians 4:2). The chief facilitator of these virtues however, is still our helper, the Holy Spirit, for without Him we can do nothing (John 15:5). He is the one who equips, rewards, and also brings about the desired result or increase (John 15:16; 1 Corinthians 3:7; Hebrews 6:10).

Luke 22:27 says, "For who is greater, he who sits at the table, or he who serves? Is it not he who sits at the table? Yet I am among you as the One who serves." This was Christ's reaction to the disciples' argument on greatness while all were at table. Greatness in the world is based on power and public recognition, but Christ taught that spiritual greatness requires humility and self-sacrifice. Jesus is our example because He came among us as the One who serves.

NO ALTERNATIVE TO SMALL GROUPS

It is important to wrap up our discussion on small groups by noting that small groups should never be just an elective in a church; nor should it merely be one extra thing we do. It is what a church must have – otherwise, we will not be able to reap abundant harvests; and even if we manage to, we will not be able to preserve them. It is not good for a member to be left to drift in the crowd alone and aimlessly. It ultimately proves detrimental, not only to such a member but the church as a whole.

Moreover, where small groups exist, our primary focus must be on regular study and practical application of the word of God in dealing with the everyday issues of life. As this happens, the groups will flourish and we will experience salvation of souls in unusual ways and unexpected places.

Prayers, in our small groups, should be administered with personal touches that are tailored to the individual needs of members, such that cannot be handled in the regular Sunday service environment. Most importantly, small groups should be forums where members interact with others and are adequately mentored, and also meet the spiritual, physical, and emotional needs of the brethren. This way, the church at large will eventually experience tremendous growth in all areas of its existence.

Chapter 5

KINGDOM WORKERS' ACCOUNTABILITY

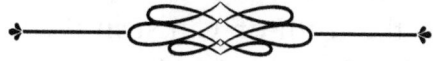

"At the end of the day, all we can do is make the best decisions we can, knowing that the final verdict will not come from shareholders, board members, church members, or even historians, but from God." - ALBERT MOHLER

The New Testament teaches about church government, church discipline, covenant commitment and mutual accountability. Philippians 1:27 says, "Only let your conduct be worthy of the gospel of Christ, so that whether I come and see you or am absent, I may hear of your affairs, that you stand fast in one spirit, with one mind striving together for the faith of the gospel."

Paul, here, reminds the church of its higher citizenship

(in the Kingdom of God), stressing that his primary concern is that they stand fast in one spirit, with a military mindset. Covenant church membership is an effective and wise path to walking together in obedience to the Lord and in a manner that is worthy of the gospel of Christ.

Church membership involves holding each other accountable to walk in a manner pleasing to God as witnesses to the truth of Christ in the world. Local church membership also involves a commitment to worshipping the Lord corporately, cooperating in mission, as well as edifying the brethren through mutual exhortation and service.

MEMBERSHIP AND MUTUAL ACCOUNTABILITY

The New Testament teaching stipulates that the local church should select qualified leaders. It also specifies affirmation of such leadership, as well as submission to the leadership, based on a membership of accountability.

The local church administration consists of elders or overseers who perform the following functions:

- Equipping members – Ephesians 4:11
- Caring for members – Acts 20:28

- Teaching the word to members – 1 Tim. 3:2; Titus 1:9
- Functioning as servant-leaders (not overbearing) – Luke 23:26
- Seeing leadership as a divine call to serve – Acts 20:28
- Making the Lord the final authority in all decisions – 1 Corinthians 5:4, Acts 6:3.

Church members are to respect and reverence appointed leaders for mutual maintenance of the church's activities (1 Thessalonians 5:12). They must be submissive to them and demonstrate a teachable spirit (Hebrews 13:17). However, these leaders should not replace Christ in their hearts (Matthew 23:8-12) and must not be treated as infallible (1 Timothy 5:20).

Basically, it is assumed that there is an existence of "church membership" that consists in a corporate life of mutual accountability, leadership and submission. The whole set-up of the leaders, and people who affirm leadership will only be applicable when based on accountability of church membership.

CHURCH DISCIPLINE

The fact remains in practice that you can never find a perfect church in this age. As imperfect beings, we are still prone to sinning after conversion and being born again. Therefore, the church is simply a company of forgiven sinners who wrestle and constantly battle against sinful desires every day.

Church membership does not imply perfect living. It is rather a commitment to worshipping God and ministering in a congregation of a local or universal church of believers where the members operate on a mutual covenant to hold each other accountable to obeying what the Scripture teaches. 1 John 1:8-10 says, "If we say that we have no sin, we deceive ourselves, and the truth is not in us. If we confess our sins, He is faithful and just to forgive us our sins and to cleanse us from all unrighteousness. If we say that we have not sinned, we make Him a liar, and His word is not in us."

Note that confessing our sins does not mean a shallow recitation of misdeeds; it means owning up to and forsaking wrongdoing, as well as bringing our lives into conformity with God's goodness and commandments. God can forgive and cleanse us from all transgressions.

Paul, in Philippians 3:12-13, says, "Not that I have already attained, or am already perfected; but I press on, that I may lay hold of that for which Christ Jesus has also laid hold of me. Brethren, I do not count myself to have apprehended; but one thing I do, forgetting those things which are behind and reaching forward to those things which are ahead."

Paul clearly acknowledged his imperfection and the need for growth. His hope was to be made perfect and obtain complete salvation, in the process of pressing toward the goal, which is eternity. This should be our goal as well. However, it must be emphasized that in our journey to perfection and heaven, the place of discipline cannot be overlooked. As the Scripture says in Hebrews 12:7-8, "If you endure chastening, God deals with you as with sons; for what son is there whom a father does not chasten? But if you are without chastening, of which all have become partakers, then you are illegitimate and not sons."

In the church family, or biological family, discipline should be quite acceptable, encouraging and instructive. A well-disciplined home for a child would be where he or she is taught systematically how to make his bed through patient instruction. Nevertheless, spankings will probably be a needed part in an atmosphere of loving admonition and patient instruction, particularly in the younger years. Consequently, affirming mutual accountability should be instructive and appropriate for maintaining needed discipline in the church membership.

The implication is that all of us in the church are responsible both to give and receive counsel, consolation, encouragement, exhortation, and admonition (2 Corinthians 1:3; Hebrews 3:13; Galatians

6:11; 1 Thessalonians 5:14). 1 Thessalonians 5:14-15 exhorts, "Now we exhort you, brethren, warn those who are unruly, comfort the fainthearted, uphold the weak, be patient with all. See that no one renders evil for evil to anyone, but always pursue what is good both for yourselves and for all."

Church members should mutually manifest mutual discipline and be sure to recognize, respect and have high esteem for the authority and work of the church leaders. Paul's instruction also reflects back on Jesus' teaching not to follow a retaliatory "eye for eye" ethic but to give a blessing instead (Matthew 5:38-42). Membership in the church is thus a commitment to the tender love of encouragement, coupled with a tough love of confrontation - to give it humbly and to receive it without defensiveness.

This concept is established in the New Testament church doctrine as follows:

1. Doctrine of the priesthood of all believers – (1 Peter 2:5,9; Revelation 1:6; 5:10)

2. We are priests and minister God's grace to each other – (1 Peter 4:10)

3. We intercede for one another before God – (Romans 15:30)

4. We confess our sins to each other – (James 5:16)

DISCIPLINARY ACTIONS IN THE CHURCH

What kind of disciplinary action should be applied when a member forsakes the covenant and continues to live in willful sin? Consider a scenario in which the sin of a member is open to the public and is persistent. The commitment to pursue obedience is disregarded; instead of pursuing obedience, the member continues to show no remorse for sinning. Resolution of such a case would involve engaging those members who are the nearest friends to approach the person early in his or her slide to sin. In the absence of repentance, the process of Matthew 18:15-17 should continue to be followed. However, the goal at every step of the way is repentance, reconciliation, and forgiveness for the good of the offender, and the spiritual health of the church to the glory of Christ.

The fact that it is pretty easy nowadays (due to proliferation of churches) for a disciplined person to be offended and withdraw to another church should not compromise or hinder the obedience of the church.

In managing offences among one another, Matthew 18:15-17 states, "Moreover if your brother sins against you, go and tell him his fault between you and him alone. If he hears you, you have gained your brother. But if he will not hear, take with you one or two more, that by the mouth of two or three witnesses every word may be established.' And if he refuses to hear them, tell it to the church. But if he refuses even to hear the church, let him be to you like a heathen and a tax collector."

These verses outline the process by which disciples demonstrate the Great Shepherd's concern for the stray sheep. The purpose of the process is not to punish, but to restore the sinful disciple (you have gained your brother). If, at the final step of the process, the professing disciple refuses to heed the church's call to repentance, the church must assume that such is not a true believer and must exclude him or her from fellowship (1 Corinthians 5:1-13).

BENEFITS OF CHURCH DISCIPLINE

Church discipline is almost extinct in many congregations today, perhaps because of the fear of "hurting" fellow believers or losing church membership. In certain instances, it is often because the church leadership itself is already compromised and no longer has the moral courage or spiritual stamina to enforce discipline. Whatever the case is, lack of discipline has contributed significantly to the death of many churches, as well as the palpable absence of the power of God in some others that are physically existing but spiritually dead.

Christ tells the church in Thyrathira: "I know your works, love, service, faith, and your patience... Nevertheless I have a few things against you, because you allow that woman Jezebel, who calls herself a prophetess, to teach and seduce My servants to commit sexual immorality and eat things sacrificed to idols..." (Revelation 2:18-29). It is to avoid such verdicts as this and to keep our churches pure and flourishing with God's glory that we must apply the rod of discipline when necessary.

Mark Dever has outline five benefits of church discipline that requires our utmost attention as we conclude this chapter:

1. Church discipline calls a professing believer out of sin. For instance, a man in the Corinthian church was having an affair with his father's wife, and the church approved of it. Paul commanded the church to exclude the man so that the man might repent, be saved, and come back to the church (1 Corinthians 5:5).

2. Church discipline warns other Christians about the danger of sin. Paul told Timothy that if a leader sins, he should be rebuked publicly "so that the rest may stand in fear" (1 Timothy 5:20).

3. Church discipline purifies the church as a whole. Paul writes, "Do you not know that a little leaven

leavens the whole lump?" (1 Corinthians 5:7). Excommunicating an unrepentant member keeps sin's destructive influence from spreading and results in a purer, holier, healthier church.

4. Church discipline presents non-Christians with a more faithful corporate witness. Would you be surprised to learn that church discipline can be a powerful evangelistic tool? When a whole community lives in a way that's radically different from the world, people notice and wonder why (Matthew 5:16, John 13:34-35).

5. Church discipline promotes the glory of God. Christians should be conspicuously holy, not for our own reputation but for God's (1 Peter 2:12). As the church increasingly reflects God's loving and holy character, we put God's glory on display for all to see. Like a billboard! This is why God made us (Genesis 1:27, Isaiah 43:6-7, Ephesians 3:10)!

All these require our faithfulness, commitment and accountability to God as we strive to keep the church of God holy and ever ready for Christ's coming.

CHAPTER 6

CHRIST'S RESURRECTION AND THE CHURCH

"The resurrection is not merely important to the historic Christian faith; without it, there would be no Christianity. It is the singular doctrine that elevates Christianity above all other world religions." - HANK HANEGRAAFF

The Easter season is very important in the Christian world and religiously acknowledged annually, being that time of the year when we celebrate the death and resurrection of our Lord Jesus Christ. Beyond the celebration however, it is important for every believer to understand what the resurrection means, as well as its implications for the individual believer and Christendom as a whole.

Apostle Paul in Philippians 3:8-11 states, "Yet indeed

I also count all things loss for the excellence of the knowledge of Christ Jesus my Lord, for whom I have suffered the loss of all things, and count them as rubbish, that I may gain Christ and be found in Him, not having my own righteousness, which is from the law, but that which is through faith in Christ, the righteousness which is from God by faith; that I may know Him and the power of His resurrection, and the fellowship of His sufferings, being conformed to His death, if, by any means, I may attain to the resurrection from the dead."

Here, the apostle described his new aspirations in three ways. First, "found in Him" refers to the judgment day. Second, Christ gives us a "righteousness" which is through "faith" (inputted) and not from works of the law (Philippians 3:6). To "know Him" (personally, experientially) parallels and explains "found in Him". Third, this involves experiencing the power of His resurrection. Identification with Christ's sufferings brings conformity to Jesus' death through refining obedience, ultimately resulting in our own resurrection.

The single most important reason for Christ's resurrection of believers is the truth that it is the foundation of our faith. The Apostle Paul wrote that if there is no resurrection, then we are all just wasting our time away with our Christian faith. He says in 1 Corinthians 15:12-19, "Now if Christ is preached that He has been raised from the dead, how do some among you say that there is no resurrection of the dead?...For if the dead do not rise, then Christ is not risen. And if Christ is not risen, your faith is futile; you are still in your sins! Then also those who have fallen asleep in Christ have perished. If in this life only we have hope in Christ, we are of all men the most pitiable."

If Christ were not raised, then the apostolic preaching of the resurrection was without foundation, the Corinthians faith was void, and the apostles were liars. "Faith" here refers to the content of the gospel message and is synonymous with a system of beliefs. Christians should be pitied more than anyone if there is no resurrection, for in which case, we would have placed all our hopes in a falsehood.

Christianity is foundationally about the resurrection, with faith in Christ as focus for the remission of our sins and salvation of our souls. The central goal of God's plan is to redeem us from sin and death and give us a new life. Romans 6:4-7 states, "Therefore we were buried with Him through baptism into death, that just as Christ was raised from the dead by the glory of the Father, even so we also should walk in newness of life. For if we have been united together in the likeness of His death, certainly we also shall be in the likeness of His resurrection, knowing this, that our old man was crucified with Him, that the body of sin might be done away with, that we should no longer be slaves of sin. For he who has died has been freed from sin."

Despite that believers have not yet experienced resurrection, we are confident of this future reality by the fact that Christ, in whose death we share, has been raised from the death. Our old man was all we were before we became born again. The new man, in contrast, is what we are once we became born again (Ephesians 4:22-24; Colossians 3:9-10).

The new man, however, is not perfect, as we are still prone to sinning because we have indwelling sin in our mortal bodies (Romans 7:13-25), but we are in the process of renewal (Ephesians 4; Colossians 3). We cannot live as we once did because the "old man" was crucified with Christ, and in Christ the believer is a "new creation" (2 Corinthians 5:17). Sin (personified) surely has no claim over a dead person and can claim no loyalty from him.

Resurrection is the believer's ultimate hope for the future (1 Thessalonians 4:13-14; Romans 8:21-23). 1 Thessalonians 4:13-14 says, "But I do not want you to be ignorant, brethren, concerning those who have fallen asleep, lest you sorrow as others who have no hope. For if we believe that Jesus died and rose again, even so God will bring with Him those who sleep in Jesus.".

This statement is on the anticipation, hope and comfort of Christ's coming for the redemption of believers. The term "asleep", used for Christians who have died, conveys the image of a sleeping person who expects to rise up in the morning. Christians who have died will experience a bodily resurrection and will rise up once again (1 Thessalonians 4:16; John 11:11). However, until this happens to deceased believers, to be out of the body is to be at home with the Lord (2 Corinthians 5:8).

Paul further taught that the dead in Christ will rise first (1 Thessalonians 4:16). In contrast to unbelievers who hopelessly grieve over the loss of their loved ones, a believer can grieve with hope because of the future glorious resurrection (1 Thessalonians 4:18). Moreover, Jesus' resurrection reveals to believers what it will be like for us at the final resurrection (Luke 24:36-43).

WHAT IS THE RESURRECTION?

Naturally, human beings are spirits having physical bodies. The natural human body is God's creation from the foundation of the earth. Genesis 2:7 states, "And the Lord God formed man of the dust of the ground, and breathed into his nostrils the breath of life; and man became a living being." God acts here as the divine potter, skillfully fashioning man out of the dust of the ground. It is noteworthy that it was only when God breathed into the man's nostrils the breath of life that Adam became a living being.

God is Spirit (John 4:24), thus when God breathed into Adam, he and all his descendants became a unique mix of the physical and the spiritual. The Hebrew phrase "living being" is used to describe living creatures (Genesis 1:20, 24, 30; 9:12). Human beings are in a class by themselves since they alone are made in God's image.

The natural body of human beings later became corrupted by the sin of Adam and therefore doomed to die. Romans 5:12 says, "Therefore, just as through one man sin entered the world, and death through sin, and thus death spread to all men, because all sinned."

Jesus came as a regular human being but without sin, so that he could overcome the power of sin and death through resurrection, and pave way for us to do the same. Hebrews 2:14-15 states, "Inasmuch then as the children have partaken of flesh and blood, He Himself likewise shared in the same, that through death He might destroy him who had the power of death, that is, the devil, and release those who through fear of death were all their lifetime subject to bondage."

Jesus the eternal Son became a man, firstly, for it was appropriate that the Son should have a ministry completed in sufferings, which all humans experience, so that He might identify with us and bring many sons into the presence of God. Second, the Son became a man and suffered death so that He could destroy the devil and thereby free children of God from the fear of death. Third, the Son became a man and suffered death so that He could serve as a faithful High Priest in service to God. It is by reason of His faithfulness as a man who was tempted and suffered that He could make propitiation. He also suffered divine retribution on our behalf, and He is able to help us because He is like His brethren in every way, except that He is without sin.

Jesus is the firstborn of many siblings, and His example is the perfect and ultimate role model of what we believers should emulate. Romans 8:29 says, "For whom He foreknew, He also predestined to be conformed to the image of His Son, that He might be the firstborn among many brethren."

Since God has a plan that spans from eternity past to eternity future, those He foreknew refer to those whom God set His electing love upon in eternity past. Predestined means that God planned from eternity that those He foreknew would become like Christ through spiritual rebirth.

THE RESURRECTION AND OUR PHYSICAL BODIES

Since Jesus Christ is the firstborn of many siblings, we will follow His path and appear like Him. When Jesus rose at resurrection, He had a new physical body. Luke 24: 36-39 states, "Now as they said these things, Jesus Himself stood in the midst of them, and said to them, "Peace to you." But they were terrified and frightened, and supposed they had seen a spirit. And He said to them, "Why are you troubled? And why do doubts arise in your hearts? Behold My hands and My feet, that it is I Myself. Handle Me and see, for a spirit does not have flesh and bones as you see I have."

Jesus mysteriously appeared to His disciples as they were swapping stories about His several appearances that day. They were terrified, thinking they were seeing a ghost, but their fear was understandable since Jesus appeared suddenly in the middle of a crowd in a locked room. Jesus calmed the fears and doubts of His disciples with evidence of His resurrection body. The nail scars were clearly visible in His hands and feet, while the disciples could touch Him and verify that He had a human body and that He was not a spirit. Thomas even had to touch the scars physically to believe it. John 20:24-29 states, "Now Thomas, called the Twin, one of the twelve, was not with them when Jesus came. The other disciples therefore said to him, "We have seen the Lord." So he said to them, "Unless I see in His hands the print of the nails, and put my finger into the print of the nails, and put my hand into His side, I will not believe." And after eight days His disciples were again inside, and Thomas with them. Jesus came, the doors being shut, and stood in the midst, and said, "Peace to you!" Then He said to Thomas, "Reach your finger here, and look at My hands; and reach your hand here, and put it into My side. Do not be unbelieving, but believing." And Thomas answered and said to Him, "My Lord and my God!" Jesus said to him, "Thomas, because you have seen Me, you have believed. Blessed are those who have not seen and yet have believed."

Apparently, Thomas initially thought the disciples had seen a ghost (Matthew 14:26). However, John reveals and affirms that Jesus' resurrection body was not a phantom or spirit apparition, but a genuine (glorified) human body (John 20:27). John has written the truth about God's Son through the Holy Spirit, thus readers of the Gospel of John would believe without seeing.

Job also testified of the resurrection of his physical body. Job 19:25-27 states, "For I know that my Redeemer lives, And He shall stand at last on the earth; And after my skin is destroyed, this I know, That in my flesh I shall see God, Whom I shall see for myself, And my eyes shall behold, and not another. How my heart yearns within me!"

Job was confident that, if he were to die, the living God would stand on the earth of his grave and testify on his behalf. Although he would lie in the grave (Job 19:25), with his body decayed, he would personally see God. Interestingly, Job had earlier expressed the fond hope of a personal life after death (Job 14:14-15).

Paul also says the body is raised in incorruption, referring to a glorious body. 1 Corinthians 15:42 states, "So also is the resurrection of the dead. The body is sown in corruption, it is raised in incorruption." Having reviewed differentiations within the created order, Paul teaches on differentiations of the resurrected body. The body changes from a perishable body (a natural body) to a glorious, imperishable body (a spiritual body) though one that has physical characteristics (see Luke 24:39).

Note that this glorious body is not in any way like a reincarnation at all! Jesus didn't become a different person after he rose from the dead. His disciples and even doubting Thomas identified him correctly and recognized his facial traits and bodily features beyond any iota of doubt. Job also testified that he would still be same person in the resurrection (Job 19:27). Though this earthly body will die, our spirit and soul will not. The Bible says it's like putting on a new suit, or getting a big upgrade (1 Corinthians 15:53-54).

ATTRIBUTES OF OUR RESURRECTED BODY

Our new bodies will be immortal and immune to sickness and disease. 1 Corinthians 15:53-54 states, "For this corruptible must put on incorruption, and this mortal must put on immortality. So when this corruptible has put on incorruption, and this mortal has put on immortality, then shall be brought to pass the saying that is written: "Death is swallowed up in victory."

The body that bears the image of the man of dust (the first Adam) must inevitably be changed into the incorruption and immortality of the body that bears the image of the man from heaven (the second Adam). The exchange of corruption for incorruption comes from when death and corruption are swallowed up by Jesus Christ (Isaiah 25:8; Hosea 13:14).

Believers are with the Lord immediately after death (see Luke 23:43; Acts 7:55-59; 2 Corinthians 5:1-8). Our new bodies will not be natural, but celestial (1 Corinthians 15:40, 44). Happily and cheeringly, we will look like Jesus. Hallelujah! (Psalm 17:15; 1 John 3:2). 1 John 3:2 says, "Beloved, now we are children of God; and it has not yet been revealed what we shall be, but we know that when He is revealed, we shall be like Him, for we shall see Him as He is."

John reminds Christians that we are what we are because God has loved us (1 John 4:10). The world may think little of us now, but at Christ's return, things will change, as believers will be transformed.

OUR APPEARANCE IN HEAVEN WITH THE LORD

When our physical body dies on earth, our spirit is with the Lord in heaven, while we await our new bodies. At rapture, when the trumpet sounds, those who are "asleep" (dead in Christ) will wake up and receive their new bodies; then the rest of us who are still alive get ours and follow them to heaven. The Bible makes it clear that everything gets to be redeemed, and that God is also going to create a new earth for us! (2 Peter 3:13; Romans 8:19-23; Revelation 21:13).

2 Peter 3:13 states, "Nevertheless we, according to His promise, look for new heavens and a new earth in which righteousness dwells." The anticipation of the Lord's return (The Day of the Lord) and its accompanying events of judgment should rouse Christians to holy living. Righteousness will permanently dwell in the new heavens and the new earth (Isaiah 32:16).

When Christ returns, evil will be completely destroyed. Revelation 21:1-5 narrates, "Now I saw a new heaven and a new earth, for the first heaven and the first earth had passed away. Also there was no more sea. Then I, John, saw the holy city, New Jerusalem, coming down out of heaven from God, prepared as a bride adorned for her husband. And I heard a loud voice from heaven saying, "Behold, the tabernacle of God is with men, and He will dwell with them, and they shall be His people. God Himself will be with them and be their God. And God will wipe away every tear from their eyes; there shall be no more death, nor sorrow, nor crying. There shall be no more pain, for the former things have passed away." Then He who sat on the throne said, "Behold, I make all things new." And He said to me, "Write, for these words are true and faithful."

All things will be made new. While the present creation is same always, the new heaven and the new earth will be much different. For example, there shall be no sea in the new creation. The Holy City, New Jerusalem, is pictured as the bride of the Lamb. The expression "coming down of heaven" is used to imply that the New Jerusalem will be suspended in the air, slightly above the new earth. "Prepared…adorned" means that the bride will be just as beautiful, and will maintain this beauty for eternity, as she will be during the wedding festivities (Revelation 19:7-8). God's arrival and presence will totally blot out death and pain, while all things will get redeemed in all ramifications. Hallelujah!!!

CONSOLATIONS IN OUR PRESENT STATE

For the born-again Christian still here on earth, the reassuring consolation is that you already have a new spirit that is made in the image of God. You can therefore, walk in the power of the resurrection by faith in Christ – power over sin, sickness and even death. Romans 8:11 says, "But if the Spirit of Him who raised Jesus from the dead dwells in you, He who raised Christ from the dead will also give life to your mortal bodies through His Spirit who dwells in you."

Since the Spirit dwells in us as believers, we exist and function in a new realm. Notwithstanding, our physical body will still die because of sin effect (unless the Lord returns before death; 1 Corinthians 15:50-57). The Spirit provides life and righteousness, and the pledge and promise of the Spirit is that He will raise us as He did Jesus.

The Christian is activated by the Holy Spirit to decisively subdue the flesh and its vain weaknesses, and live. The leading of the Spirit of God is His providential sanctification (Psalm 23:3) that will bring the believer to glory (Romans 8:17). The leading of the Spirit of God is the Spirit's empowerment for mortification of worldly and fleshly desires.

Invariably, you get to enjoy some Kingdom benefits now, because you already have your citizenship from heaven (Philippians 3:20; Colossians 1:12-14; Ephesians 1:3,7). Ephesians 1:3,7 states, "Blessed be the God and Father of our Lord Jesus Christ, who has blessed us with every spiritual blessing in the heavenly places in Christ...In Him we have redemption through His blood, the forgiveness of sins, according to the riches of His grace."

Every marvelous spiritual blessing is gifted to each believer in the church in Jesus Christ, for they flow from God's grace, wisdom and eternal purpose. These blessings include our salvation, being seated with Christ in the heavenly places, our redemption, adoption and election. Believers have been bought with the price of Christ's blood (1 Peter 1:18-19; 1 Corinthians 6:20; 1 Timothy 2:6). We have been redeemed from Satan, sin, and the misery of sinful self. The result of our redemption is the banishment of our sin debt, resulting in complete forgiveness.

Just in case you are not born again, here's an opportunity to get on board right away. Simply acknowledge your sins to God, repent and ask Jesus to come into your heart today. It is that easy to invite and accept Jesus into your life as author and finisher of your faith. Only believe, and you will be saved; for "if the Son makes you free, you shall be free indeed" (John 8:36).

CHAPTER 7

THE PRICE OF OUR REDEMPTION

"Christ is the very epitome of innocence, and without the blood of Christ, shed on Calvary, God's plan of salvation would not have been fulfilled." —ALAN KEYES

The epistle to the Hebrews is a tribute to the incomparable Son of God, and source of encouragement to persecuted believers. Jesus Christ is exalted as both "God" and "this man", and thus the only One who can serve as Mediator between God and man, while fellow Christians are exhorted to go on to perfection and live by faith.

Hebrews is a written theological sermon that discloses the broad sweep of God's grand redemption plan for humanity. Hebrews 9:11-14 says, "But Christ came as High Priest of the good things to come, with the greater and more perfect tabernacle not made with hands, that is, not of this creation. Not with the blood of goats and calves, but with His own blood He entered the Most Holy Place once for all, having obtained eternal redemption. For if the blood of bulls and goats and the ashes of a heifer, sprinkling the unclean, sanctifies for the purifying of the flesh, how much more shall the blood of Christ, who through the eternal Spirit offered Himself without spot to God, cleanse your conscience from dead works to serve the living God?"

Jesus is upheld as the final sacrifice and the only One who can serve as mediator between God and man. The once-and-for-all bodily sacrifice of Jesus in His redemptive process, in conformity with the will of God, supersedes all other offerings. Hebrews 9:22 states, "And according to the law almost all things are purified with blood, and without shedding of blood there is no remission"; while Hebrews 10:4 declares, "For it is not possible that the blood of bulls and goats could take away sins."

The blood sacrifices offered by the law were inadequate, useless, and condemned. Therefore, Jesus' death on the cross, being a covenant sacrifice, is sufficient, superior, and of eternal permanence for atonement of our sins. Hallelujah!

SUPREMACY OF THE NEW PRIESTHOOD

The Old Testament priesthood involved the ordinances of divine service given through the old covenant which were for an earthly sanctuary that represented the transcendence of God. But the people could not enter the sanctuary in the tabernacle. Only the High Priest could enter the holiest place, which he did only once a year. The sacrificial ministry of the old priesthood was not capable of making perfect the worshippers' conscience, and thus incomplete.

However, the sacrificial ministry of the Messiah is able to cleanse our conscience. This perfect cleansing enables followers of the Messiah to engage in works that serve the living God. The ministry of the Messiah is that of a new covenant mediator. It is superior because He does not enter an earthly sanctuary, but into heaven itself, and thus into the very presence of God.

The unique fact is that the Messiah entered into the Most Holy Place once and for all, unlike the high priest who entered annually into the Most Holy Place. Unlike the old covenant that was inaugurated by the death of animals that had no choice in the matter, the new covenant was inaugurated by the Messiah's voluntary death. The Messiah offered His own blood, unlike the priesthood that offered the blood of animals. Unlike the old priesthood that offered sacrifices continually without effect, the blood of the Messiah obtained eternal redemption for us.

The old sacrifices were only a shadow of the very image of the blessed realities that would come from the personal sacrifice of the Messiah. God was no longer interested in the burnt offerings and sacrifices for sin of the old covenant (Psalm 40:6-8). The old sacrifices had to be offered continually, and they did not accomplish much beyond ritual purification because they could not take away sins or blot out transgressions. This was the reason the prophecy came that the Messiah would come to do God's will.

Jesus, the Messiah, then offered one sacrifice for sins forever, by offering Himself, and later sat down at the throne of God. He offered the perfect sacrifice that perfected believers, and because of His blood of atonement, the old sacrifices were no longer necessary.

WHY JESUS' BLOOD IS THE PERFECT SACRIFICE

1. The blood of Jesus has taken away our sins – Hebrews 10:12.

2. It put an end to sacrifices (including past and future ones) – Hebrews 10:18.

3. Jesus did what could not be done by the law – Hebrews 1:1-8.

4. Jesus is the will of God by design – Hebrews 10:7, 9-10.

5. The blood of Jesus abolished the old covenant – Hebrews 10:1,9.

6. The blood of Jesus brought forgiveness of sins – Ephesians 1:7; Hebrews 10:17.

7. The blood of Jesus established a new covenant – Hebrews 10:1, 16.

8. The sacrifice of Jesus has permanently cleansed our consciences – Hebrews 10:22.

9. The blood of Jesus has perfected those who are sanctified – Hebrews 10:13.

10. Christ's atonement has made God's law to be written on our hearts and in our minds – Hebrews 10:16.

HOW THE BLOOD OF JESUS EMPOWERS BELIEVERS

- **We are able to conquer the accuser of the brethren.**

Revelation 12:11 states, "And they overcame him

by the blood of the Lamb and by the word of their testimony, and they did not love their lives to the death.". Sometimes what looks like defeat is victory, as when believers die for their faith. Satan has killed them, but they are the ultimate victors because of the blood of the Lamb (Christ's death on the cross) and the word of their testimony. Because Satan has been banned from heaven, the heavens and those who dwell in them can rejoice.

In view of this ultimate triumph that awaits us, Christians must strive daily toward peace and holiness, and they should warn one another against falling short of God's grace or allowing any root of bitterness to spring up within them. Hebrews 12:14-15 says, "Pursue peace with all people, and holiness, without which no one will see the Lord: looking carefully lest anyone fall short of the grace of God; lest any root of bitterness springing up cause trouble, and by this many become defiled."

The church does not exist on Mount Sinai with its terrifying law that commands and condemns. Rather, the church is moving toward Mount Zion where it will dwell in the presence of God, Jesus, angels and the righteous people who have been perfected by the sprinkled blood of Christ.

- **Believers gain access to God in worship and prayer** (Ephesians 2:13; 6:18; Colossians 1:21; Psalm 62:8).

Ephesians 6:18-20 states, "praying always with all prayer and supplication in the Spirit, being watchful to this end with all perseverance and supplication for all the saints— and for me, that utterance may be given to me, that I may open my mouth boldly to make known the mystery of the gospel, for which I am an ambassador in chains; that in it I may speak boldly, as I ought to speak."

Paul called believers to put on the "whole armor of God" (Ephesians 6:13). He describes five defensive components of the armor and one offensive weapon - a short sword used in close combat, symbolizing the word of God. The Scripture can be described as "faithful" because of its design, content, and origin (2 Timothy 2:11), confirmed (Hebrews 2:3; 2 Peter 1:19), and enduring forever (1 Peter 1:24-25).

Each component of the divine armor must be carefully put on with prayer, drawing upon divine resources. This prayer is Spirit-energized, Spirit-enabled, and spirit-directed. Praying in the spirit is an admission of a believer's ignorance and total dependence on God as our ultimate defender.

- **Believers are rescued from the power of sin by the empowerment of the blood of Jesus.**

1 Peter 1:18-19 states, "Knowing that you were not redeemed with corruptible things, like silver or gold, from your aimless conduct received by tradition from your fathers, but with the precious blood of Christ, as of a lamb without blemish and without spot."

God is the Christian's standard for holy living, and the metaphor "a lamb without blemish and without spot" refers to Christ's total sinlessness (Leviticus 22:19-25). He is the sacrificial pure Lamb of God (John 1:29; Revelation 9:5). The plan for Christ's sacrifice on behalf of sinners was fixed in eternity past, a sure reality set to unfold at a divinely appointed time in history (Galatians 4:4).

- **Believers are progressively cleansed from more and more sin.**

Hebrews 13:12 reveals, "Therefore Jesus also, that He might sanctify the people with His own blood, suffered outside the gate." The benefits and responsibilities of life lived in the church should reflect in progressive cleansing of the believer's sinful life. One of the manifestations of continual improvement in believers' spiritual life includes ways in which they should revere church leaders, such as imitating their faith; judging every teaching according to the gospel; ignoring world's spiteful attitude towards believers; confessing the name of Christ in appreciation always; being active in doing good works; obeying and submitting to leaders in authority; and praying for their leaders to have clear consciences, conducting themselves with honor in everything.

WONDERS OF THE BLOOD OF JESUS

1. It is the means by which Jesus purchased the church – Acts 20:38.

2. It causes us to dwell in Christ and He in us – John 6:56.

3. It is the means by which Jesus becomes our atonement through faith – Romans 3:25.

4. It has obtained eternal redemption for us – Hebrews 9:12.

5. It justifies and saves us from wrath – Romans 5:9.

6. It brings reconciliation with God and inner peace – Colossians 1:20.

7. It remits sins – Matthew 26:28.

8. It gives life to those who consumes it – John 6:53.

9. It sanctified us – Hebrews 13:2.

10. It gives us continuous victory over Satan and all his works.

PLUNGE INTO THE BLOOD!

The blood of Jesus Christ is superior, sufficient, and permanent, being a covenant sacrifice that replaces the old covenant with righteousness and brings eternal security. Christ's redemptive process finally made us holy, removed us from sin, destroyed our enemy, and provided us with eternal life.

The Lord Jesus has created a powerful bond between Him and us with His blood sacrifice. We are cemented to the Lord, locked by His determined love and relationship, and nothing can separate us from God's love. Romans 8:38-39 affirms, "For I am persuaded that neither death nor life, nor angels nor principalities nor powers, nor things present nor things to come, nor height nor depth, nor any other created thing, shall be able to separate us from the love of God which is in Christ Jesus our Lord."

Jesus conquered death and Satan on the cross, ensuring that nothing can change God's love or purpose for us. We are kept by the power of God through faith for salvation ready to be revealed in the last time (1 Peter 1:5).

Chapter 8

POWER IN THE NAME OF JESUS

> *"To holy people, the very name of Jesus is a name to feed upon, a name to transport. His name can raise the dead and transfigure and beautify the living."*
> —John Henry Newman

Your name is everything you represent and is your person in all ramifications. There is an old adage that no matter what you do, the name given to you at birth and by which you are called thereafter eventually manifests and trails your life. Your name can say a lot about you. For instance, the name of a king represents his honor, crown, jurisdiction, territorial integrity, power, and so on.

This also applies to the name of Jesus. In fact, Billy Sunday, the renowned evangelist, once said in one of his sermons, "There are two hundred and fifty-six names given in the Bible for the Lord Jesus Christ, and I suppose this was because He was infinitely beyond all that any one name could express."

We read in the Scripture, over and over again, "In my name", "In Jesus' name" or "In His name". All these are very significant. Christ Himself in Mark 16:17-18 declares, "And these signs will follow those who believe: In My name they will cast out demons; they will speak with new tongues; they will take up serpents; and if they drink anything deadly, it will by no means hurt them; they will lay hands on the sick, and they will recover."

Jesus named five miraculous signs that would follow those who believe in His name and declare it (note, not just those who preach in His name). This emphasizes that the power to do these things comes from the risen Lord. Everything we say or do successfully in God's Kingdom is through the name of Jesus. This is why the apostle exhorts in Colossians 3:17, "And whatever you do in word or deed, do all in the name of the Lord Jesus, giving thanks to God the Father through Him."

Paul showed how doing everything in the name of the Lord applies to every member of a household. Early Christians adopted and modified this format for describing appropriate behavior of members in a Christian household (see Ephesians 5:21-6:9; Titus

2:2-10; 1 Peter 2:18-3:7). Jesus has urged, invited and commanded us to pray in His name, with the assurance of incredible results. John 14:13-14 and 16:23-24 contain some of the most powerful assurances in all scriptures related to prayer. John 16:23-24 states, "And in that day you will ask Me nothing. Most assuredly, I say to you, whatever you ask the Father in My name He will give you. Until now you have asked nothing in My name. Ask, and you will receive, that your joy may be full."

Jesus is the way, the truth, and the life. He alone can turn sorrow to joy in the life of a believer. He assures us again in John 14:13-14, "And whatever you ask in My name, that I will do, that the Father may be glorified in the Son. If you ask anything in My name, I will do it." Such answered prayer is however hinged on alignment of one's desires and purposes with God's (1 John 5:14-15).

EXPLOITS IN THE NAME OF JESUS

Healing occurred in the name of Jesus. Acts 3:6 recounts, "Then Peter said, "Silver and gold I do not have, but what I do have I give you: In the name of Jesus Christ of Nazareth, rise up and walk." It is good for the lame man that Peter and John had neither gold nor silver to hand to him. Indeed, what they did have to offer was of a greater value – healing power through Jesus Christ. This lame man at the Beautiful Gate got his healing miracle in that he was given a permanent remedy for his physical and spiritual problems, rather than a temporary fix.

Testifying later about the healing miracle, Peter says in Acts 3:16, "And His name, through faith in His name, has made this man strong, whom you see and know. Yes, the faith which comes through Him has given him this perfect soundness in the presence of you all." Peter and John had a chance to claim credit (cheap popularity) for the miraculous healing of the man, but instead insisted that it was faith in Jesus' name that made the man whole. Indeed, the apostles were merely God's chosen instruments for conveying the miracle.

We are to baptize in the name of Jesus those who have received God's gift of salvation. This confirms and establishes their place in God's Kingdom. Jesus instructs us in Matthew 28:19-20, "Go therefore and make disciples of all the nations, baptizing them in the name of the Father and of the Son and of the Holy Spirit, teaching them to observe all things that I have commanded you; and lo, I am with you always, even to the end of the age." Amen."

Jesus had authority even before His resurrection

(see Matthew 7:29; 9:6,8; 11:27; 21:23). The Father, however, granted Him all authority in heaven and on earth after He had completed the work of our redemption and risen from the grave - an authority of magnitude far greater than that which Satan had vainly promised Him during His temptation (Matthew 4:10-11).

In Luke 10:18-19, we read that the devils are paralyzed at the mention of Jesus' name. Jesus, in the passage, says, "I saw Satan fall like lightning from heaven. Behold, I give you the authority to trample on serpents and scorpions, and over all the power of the enemy, and nothing shall by any means hurt you."

Part of the healing miracles performed by the seventy disciples sent out by Jesus had to do with casting out demons. The phrase "Satan fall...from heaven" (see also Ezekiel 28:16-17) refers to the initial judgment upon the devil after he rebelled against God. A further defeat was suffered by Satan as Jesus' disciples were victorious in ministry over the power of the enemy (Satan), symbolized by serpents and scorpions.

Salvation comes in the name of Jesus (Acts 4:12; Romans 10:13). Acts 4:12 states, "Nor is there salvation in any other, for there is no other name under heaven given among men by which we must be saved.". Peter made it clear that salvation from sin and reconciliation with God can only be obtained through the name of Jesus. This is the uncompromising, exclusive claim of Christianity. The same message is continually declared throughout the New Testament, while Jesus Himself says, "I am the way, the truth, and the life. No one comes to the Father except through Me" (John 14:6).

Believers are justified in the name of Jesus. 1 Corinthians 6:11 reminds us, "And such were some of you. But you were washed, but you were sanctified, but you were justified in the name of the Lord Jesus and by the Spirit of our God." Believers should not think that unbelieving judges (the unrighteous) and their worldly verdicts about serious sins can render justice in the church. These people have no inheritance in God's Kingdom. Only believers who are washed, sanctified and justified can rightly judge sin. Thus, under no circumstance should a believer sue any of the brethren to an unbeliever's law court (1 Corinthians 6:1-3). Believers shall judge the angels, how much more things that pertain to this life!

WHY THE NAME OF JESUS WORKS FOR US

1. We represent Christ's interests on earth when we pray in His name.

When most of us pray, we conclude with the phrase, "In Jesus' name". Jesus is our Mediator, Intercessor,

Advocate and Lord. Therefore, when we pray in His name, tremendous power is released. Jesus has given every believer unlimited power of attorney in all matters and with the right to use His name in every situation. It is much the same as the legal arrangement known as the power of attorney, such that one person may represent another in their absence. We act on Jesus' behalf by simply declaring His name in all matters, in alignment with God's purpose on earth.

2. We reverence and demonstrate faith in His name.

Faith and holy reverence are two major activators of the power of Jesus' name in our lives and circumstances. What this means therefore is that the name will prove powerless without sincere faith and total trust. Calling the name of Jesus in doubt, unbelief, or carelessly will certainly not work. Furthermore, it is very crucial that while we mention the name of Jesus in faith, it must be with the absolute understanding of the divine power that is loaded in His name. As Peter says it again, "And His name, through faith in His name, has made this man strong, whom you see and know. Yes, the faith which comes through Him has given him this perfect soundness in the presence of you all" (Acts 3:16).

3. We demonstrate His authority.

Imagine an unauthorized user trying to wield the authority of the state. Compare this with what happens when a recognized state official does same. The state official normally wears an emblem of authority either in uniform, costumes, badges, caps, or medals with the appropriate identification tags. The huge difference lies in the recognition of the official status of the authorized official who fully and legally represents the state in conducting or enforcing some state laws and regulations.

This is what happens to us as believers. The name of Jesus works for us because we know Him and He knows us. It goes without saying, then, that the use of Jesus' name cannot be effective if we have no relationship with Him. Spiritual oneness is critical if the use of the name is to have power with God, men or even the devil.

We must get rid of selfish agenda as users of His name, and we should always presuppose our own total, unreserved submission to His will. The name, therefore, is as powerful as we are surrendered to Him (Mark 16:17-18; Acts 3:6, 16: 4:10).

4. It is the key to receiving answers to our prayers.

The name of Jesus is the key, and He gave us the authority to use His name. Since we have authority in His name, all we have to do is use it. This can be likened to going to the bank of heaven; knowing that I have nothing deposited, going in my name will get me absolutely nothing. In contrast, Jesus Christ has unlimited deposits in heaven's bank, and He has granted me the privilege of going to the bank with His name, drawing on my "checks" (John 16:23; Philippians 2:9-10). Philippians 2:9-11 reveals, "Therefore God also has highly exalted Him and given Him the name which is above every name, that at the name of Jesus every knee should bow, of those in heaven, and of those on earth, and of those under the earth, and that every tongue should confess that Jesus Christ is Lord, to the glory of God the Father."

"God has highly exalted Him" suggests that God gave Jesus a new position, and this name that is above every name is Lord (Yahweh). The bowing and confession imply submissive reverence to Him. The jurisdiction includes all spatial dimensions in heaven, earth, and under the earth. Together, they indicate the living and the dead all bringing glory and honor to God. Jesus is the only One who qualifies to mediate between God and humans. He is the administrator of God's will on earth, and the focus of worship (Lord).

5. We have power in His name for combat.

Jesus gave us His name to battle the devil, resist him and put him on the run (1 Peter 5:8). James 4:7 says, "Therefore submit to God. Resist the devil and he will flee from you." To resist the devil suggests an active resistance against temptation. Luke 10:17 states, "Then the seventy returned with joy, saying, "Lord, even the demons are subject to us in Your name." The disciples returned with joy because they cast out demons in the name of Jesus.

On the contrary, Acts 19:14-16 reveals, "Also there were seven sons of Sceva, a Jewish chief priest, who did so. And the evil spirit answered and said, "Jesus I know, and Paul I know; but who are you?" Then the man in whom the evil spirit was leaped on them, overpowered them, and prevailed against them, so that they fled out of that house naked and wounded."

It takes more than the invocation of powerful names to gain an upper hand over demonic forces. The evil spirits recognized that the exorcists did not share in Christ's authority through faith. The consequences of frivolously invoking Jesus' name were severe. Causing the men to flee naked was especially humiliating since Jesus shunned nudity. Following the incident, people got to realize that the power of the Lord was not available for just anyone to manipulate. The name of the Lord Jesus was magnified rather than being abused.

Jesus Christ has given us all (believers) power and authority, and we have to fully recognize the power and authority we have been given in His name. Jesus has given us the power of attorney, as well as the power and authority to operate in His name. It is therefore up to us, and we have the divine responsibility to exercise the authority we have in the name of Jesus, and see Him glorify Himself in our lives.

MY FIRST PUBLIC HEALING PROMPT EXPERIENCE

Let me narrate my first public healing application by laying of hands "in the name of Jesus." The incident happened at a carwash plant on Westheimer Road in Houston, Texas. I had earlier engaged in several successful healing prayers privately at home on members of my family (wife, children, friends, grandchildren), and on some members of my church in the hallways, or in a private room. I was always shy to conduct healing on the sick in the public, due to fear of the crowd. However, I had increasingly become confident of the validity of the healing virtue in us through Jesus Christ.

I have been privileged on a number of occasions to be God's chosen instrument in conveying the miracle healing of brethren from headaches, joint pains, stomach problems and other ailments by laying of hands. However, as I earlier noted, my first healing prompt experience happened in mid-August 2018

The Living Church

at a carwash premises in Houston, Texas. I usually routinely wash my car at this particular carwash plant early in the morning before 10 am, being the deadline time for "early bird" sales reduction.

After depositing my car at the entrance of the auto washing machine, I went inside the office to make my payment. I paid as usual to the lady attendant who ran and processed my credit card for the payment. I later proceeded towards the waiting room, but hardly took two steps when I heard a cry of distress back at the payment spot. I looked back and saw the same lady attendant, who had processed my payment, screaming frantically. Her entire body shook rapidly, while she shouted to be taken home right away. Two other co-workers tried to attend to her behind the payment machine counter. I very quickly ran to them and asked her to allow me to pray for her. The co-workers initially tried to shun my gesture, but I boldly told them that she would be healed instantly if they would just allow me to pray for her. All I prayed and declared promptly was, "Be healed in the name of Jesus". I said it very loudly and boldly, with belief and conviction. Behold, the sick lady instantly calmed down, stopped crying, and all the shaking in her entire body stopped. Hallelujah!!!

All these happened very quickly in a couple of minutes, while more car wash customers had gathered to their amazement. Honestly, it was like a dream of an experience the way it was prompted. I remember saying, "Thank you, Jesus" loudly after the event. The lady went back to work and did not go home or anywhere else. She confirmed her healing after I went back a few days later.

I tried to review that experience, being my very first public application of what Jesus commanded us to do - laying hands on the sick for their healing. We had a healing prophet at our church a week prior to this incident, and he conducted series of healing sessions with our entire congregation. The prophet encouraged us (just as our Senior Pastor always does) to simply yield ourselves to be conduits of healing virtue by the authority that Jesus gave us in His name. He mentored us to always be very bold to demonstrate our belief and trust in Jesus Christ.

The prophet further narrated his experience during a healing deliverance of a woman whose son suddenly jumped out of the crowd to challenge him to let alone his mother. The prophet displayed boldness and confidence by asking the son to stay on the sideline to watch; he told him he was in charge under the divine cover of the church. Using this experience, the prophet urged us not to allow any intruder to scare us from performing public healing deliverance. I virtually derived my boldness and prompt incentive from the combined teaching and training we received from our Senior Pastor and the visiting prophet.

When we trust and obey Jesus' command to lay hands on the sick for healing, and in boldness take authority "in His name", His healing virtue is conveyed through us as God's instrument in delivering the miracle!

CHAPTER 9

FOUNDATION OF TRUE SUCCESS

"If you lack knowledge, go to school. If you lack wisdom, get on your knees! Knowledge is not wisdom. Wisdom is the proper use of knowledge." –VANCE HAVNER

God's desire is for us to excel in all areas of life. More graciously, He has made provision for all that we need to achieve this – the most important of which is wisdom. The people of the world generally have a twisted definition of wisdom since they perceive various occurrences of life from their own corrupted mindsets. James 3:13-15 explains, "Who is wise and understanding among you? Let him show by good conduct that his works are done in the meekness of wisdom. But if you have bitter envy and self-seeking in your hearts, do not boast and lie against the truth. This wisdom does not descend from above, but is earthly, sensual, demonic."

As children of God, we operate by the same fundamental divine guide (the Holy Bible). This divine manual recommends that we will only be successful when we seek and build upon knowledge, understanding and wisdom. Proverbs 4:7 says, "Wisdom is the principal thing; Therefore get wisdom. And in all your getting, get understanding" (Proverbs 4:7).

The word "get" is from the common Hebrew word for "purchase". Great emphasis is laid on wisdom and understanding as the most important acquisitions (Proverbs 16:16; 18:15; 23:23). This literally means in all your purchasing, purchase understanding; that is, spend all you can on acquiring understanding.

"Principal" means the beginning, the first thing to get. As with salvation, the cost of godly wisdom is not silver and gold. Rather, the believer must desire and pursue it above everything else.

Success has been defined as "the attainment of wealth, popularity, favor, and eminence". Charles Stanley, author of "Success, God's Way", defines success as the continuous achievement of becoming the person God wants you to be and accomplishing the goals God has purposed and helped you set for your life.

Knowledge is defined as acquired information through concerted effort, or by virtue of your location at any point in time. Understanding is the ability to discern between truthful and untruthful, helpful and unhelpful information. In other words, it is having the correct perception of a piece of information. Most importantly, wisdom is an understanding of how to deal with life and its myriad problems successfully. It involves using experience, intuition or supernatural revelation to decipher the best way to apply what you know and going ahead to apply it.

HOW TO ACQUIRE WISDOM

1. **Receive God's words and let it change you.**

James 1:22-25 states, "But be doers of the word, and not hearers only, deceiving yourselves. For if anyone is a hearer of the word and not a doer, he is like a man observing his natural face in a mirror; for he observes himself, goes away, and immediately forgets what kind of man he was. But he who looks into the perfect law of liberty and continues in it, and is not a forgetful hearer but a doer of the word, this one will be blessed in what he does."

The distinction between the hearer who forgets and the doer of the word who continues is the decision to allow the perfect law of liberty to shape one's life's course. The person who puts faith into his action is blessed; and his worship influences his life and transforms his destiny. Conversely, the person who refuses to allow the word to influence his life will continue to grope in the darkness of ignorance and foolish decisions.

2. Give attention to God's words.

Believers must keep on learning and improving progressively! A wise man will hear and increase in learning and a man of understanding will get wise counsel (Joshua 1:8; Proverbs 1:5). A man of understanding has the capacity to grasp what he hears and sees and to internalize knowledge so that it directs his actions.

Joshua 1:8 states, "This Book of the Law shall not depart from your mouth, but you shall meditate in it day and night, that you may observe to do according to all that is written in it. For then you will make your way prosperous, and then you will have good success." Two more references to the law affirm the key importance of God's revelation. Studying and meditating on it are to form so much a part of one's life that the words are fully obeyed as in Deuteronomy 6:6-9. The "frame" of God's promised presence in Joshua 1:5,9 indicates that Joshua's success will come because God is with him, enabling him to read and observe His word (Ephesians 2:8-10).

3. Seek wisdom as you search for treasures.

We must seek wisdom as we would seek treasures. Proverbs 2:4-7 exhorts, "If you seek her as silver, and search for her as for hidden treasures; then you will understand the fear of the Lord, and find the knowledge of God. For the Lord gives wisdom; from His mouth come knowledge and understanding; He stores up sound wisdom for the upright; He is a shield to those who walk uprightly."

It is not just about learning wisdom, we must first receive and internalize, rather than despise or reject it (Proverbs 1:7,30). The result of such reception and internalization of wisdom is a reverent relationship (knowledge) with God. Essentially, while we store up God's commands, He stores up sound wisdom as our reward.

We really need to be watchful as Christians to ensure we only seek godly wisdom, especially in this tumultuous world of vanity and falsehood. 1 Corinthians 2:6-8 states, "However, we speak wisdom among those who are mature, yet not the wisdom of this age, or of the rulers of this age, who are coming to nothing. But we speak of the wisdom of God in a mystery, the hidden wisdom which God ordained before the ages of our glory, which none of the rulers of this age knew; for had they known, they would not have crucified the Lord of glory."

God's supernatural wisdom was understood by those who were enabled to see it through the Spirit's illumination. A "mystery" is a former secret openly revealed by God, such as the gospel message that Christ crucified is truly the Lord of glory. The rulers of this age did not recognize Jesus as the Lord of glory. Consequently, their lack of recognition resulted in His crucifixion, and this in turn became the foundational basis of the gospel. Hallelujah!!! Our acceptance was thus made possible by Christ's rejection. "Hidden wisdom of God" refers to the deepest wisdom that God's Spirit reveals to believers, being the most profound and highest wisdom as understood that Jesus Christ is the Lord of glory, "and Him crucified."

If anyone is in need of wisdom, he should humbly ask God, for He gives liberally. James 1:5-8 assures, "If any of you lacks wisdom, let him ask of God, who gives to all liberally and without reproach, and it will be given to him. But let him ask in faith, with no doubting, for he who doubts is like a wave of the sea driven and tossed by the wind. For let not that man suppose that he will receive anything from the Lord; he is a double-minded man, unstable in all his ways."

The world's harsh treatment often tempts us to withdraw and refuse to expose our lack of wisdom for fear of being shamed by our peers, but God gives generously and without ridiculing those who ask. It is vital for a believer to ask for wisdom in faith without doubting. The basis of our confidence is not the fact that we exercise faith, but the person in whom we place our faith, the faithful and unchangeable God.

4. Embrace wisdom in your thoughts and aspirations.

As you walk the journey of life, you must keep wisdom in front of your thoughts and aspirations. As a believer, you should be conscious of the fact that God has already deposited in you all you need to achieve success in all ramifications and seek to align with His purpose for your life. Proverbs 3:21-24 states, "My son, let them not depart from your eyes—Keep sound wisdom and discretion; So they will be life to your soul and grace to your neck. Then you will walk safely in your way, and your foot will not stumble. When you lie down, you will not be afraid; Yes, you will lie down and your sleep will be sweet."

A believer must esteem wisdom and consider it as the key to life – a full life now and an eternal life in the future because it is anchored in the fear of the Lord, and it includes practical advice. Although the wicked will suddenly come to trouble at their ending (Psalm 35:8; Isaiah 10:3; 47:11; 1 Thessalonians 5:3), those who maintain wisdom (Proverbs 3:21) will never be in such danger, whether up and, about, sleeping. The faithful God will always protect them.

5. Move from knowledge to wisdom.

For you to properly grasp the implicit meaning of the wisdom of God, you need to be particularly conscious as you walk through the book of Proverbs, to identify the insights you may have acquired (KNOWLEDGE); pray fervently and ask the Holy Spirit to fill you with unction to develop a deep perception of what these words really mean (UNDERSTANDING). It is after this that you can determine how these insights could be maximized and applied to real life situations under various circumstances, including in your family home, community, among your peer groups, friends, in your workplace, and in your business dealings and transactions.

BENEFITS OF ACQUIRING WISDOM

- **Honor:** A wise man is honorable. He speaks with discretion, making others to recognize and honor him for the wisdom he displays, whereas an ignorant person is held in contempt and people despise their advice (Proverbs 3:35).

- **Long life:** Long life results from applying wisdom and knowledge to your daily life. Proverbs 4:10 counsels, "Hear, my son, and receive my sayings, And the years of your life will be many." Indeed, longevity of life, which many desperately seek these days, is easily found in the wisdom of adhering to God's instructions. For example, a commandment of God says, "Children, obey your parents in the Lord, for this is right. "Honor your father and mother," which is the first commandment with promise: "that it may be well with you and you may live long on the earth" (Ephesians 6:1-3). Many who had refused such wisdom from God's word have had their lives prematurely terminated.

- **Understanding and knowledge:** The wise always have access to treasures of knowledge (Proverbs 10:14); and they are people of uncommon understanding (Proverbs 10:13, 14:8).

- **Eminence:** A man of wisdom usually commands eminence. He is held and regarded as a person of high esteem and integrity. He is a role model and a reliable counselor.

- **True riches and profitable instruction:** These encompass all desirable things, including a happy and prosperous long life, favor from God and man, the treasures of wisdom which are hid in Jesus Christ, as well as eternal life (Proverbs 8:11, Colossians 2:3). The Bible instructs us that wisdom is better than rubies, and all the things one may desire cannot in any way be compared to wisdom.

- **Protection and safety:** Wisdom enables you to discern the wicked plans of the enemy. You will discern most of the harmful tricks of the enemy and use discretion. Proverbs 2:11-13 says, "Discretion will preserve you; Understanding will keep you, to deliver you from the way of evil, from the man who speaks perverse things, from those who leave the paths of uprightness to walk in the ways of darkness."

CONSEQUENCES OF LACK OF WISDOM

1. Self-deception and eventual frustration. Proverbs 14:8 says, "The wisdom of the prudent is to understand his way, but the folly of fools is deceit." The foolish person often embarks on a journey of mockery and self- deception because he thinks he is smarter than everyone else. Alas! His wicked plots often crash in utter disappointment.

2. Poor decision-making. When there is no wisdom, decisions often end up badly, even if they are conceived with the best intentions (Proverbs 14:12).

3. Lack of purpose and fulfillment. "A man who wanders from the way of understanding will rest in the assembly of the dead" (Proverbs 21:16). Deficiency of wisdom confines one to a place of hopelessness and torment. A believer cannot afford to live a purposeless and "walking dead" life; thus, he must continue to increase in wisdom, while refusing to wander into ignorance.

4. Risk of premature death. Proverbs 10:21 warns, "The lips of the righteous feed many, but fools die for lack of wisdom." This, certainly, is not your portion in Jesus' name.

5. Pride and an unteachable spirit. A prideful fool is easy to identify in that he detests the word of God and is not God-fearing. (Proverbs 1:7; 14:3). Proverbs 1:7 says, "The fear of the Lord is the beginning of knowledge, But fools despise wisdom and instruction."

6. Lack of endurance and self-control. Those who lack wisdom also often lack endurance. They anxiously anticipate pay-back and instant gratification, to their ultimate detriment (Hebrews 12:15-17).

7. Trail of calamity and destruction. The foolish tear down even their own works, and leave a path of calamity and broken lives in their path (Proverbs 14:1)

8. Irrational thinking and rashness in decisions. People who lack wisdom are devoid of a conscious thought process; they are never objective, and hurry over decision-making.

9. Headiness and foolhardiness. The unwise person hardly responds positively to admonishment or punishment. No matter what extra efforts you make, a fool will not try to retrace his steps or choose to see the truth. Severe punishment will not even readily make him change his mind (Proverbs 27:22).

10. Reckless and thoughtless living. Unwise people are generally out of control. They are over-sensitive and get unnecessarily emotional about everything. They carelessly say things because it feels great to say them, not caring about other people's feelings.

GO FOR WISDOM!

Now that we have seen some awesome attributes of the wise, as well as the repulsive characteristics of the foolish, it becomes apparent that the way of wisdom is the way to go. The benefits of acquiring wisdom are too delightful to ignore; while the consequences of lack of wisdom are too dreadful to ponder.

It is very vital that you familiarize yourself with and make good use of the truths that have been revealed in this chapter. This, I believe, will enable you to discern what exactly God expects from you in gaining knowledge, understanding, and wisdom.

CHAPTER 10

FASTING THAT WORKS

> *"Fasting in the biblical sense is choosing not to partake of food because your spiritual hunger is so deep, your determination in intercession so intense, or your spiritual warfare so demanding that you have temporarily set aside even fleshly needs to give yourself to prayer and meditation."* –WESLEY L. DUEWEL

The lyrics of a well-known song that is commonly delivered during fellowship prayers assert, "God who answers by fire will be our God". That God is the God of Elijah – that man of God whose prayers brought down answers by fire from heaven. However, there are certain things about that man, the circumstances that surrounded him and the pattern of his prayers that we must be familiar with, so that we do not sing or pray without understanding.

We are at the end of the age —a time in which people generally crave instant gratifications of personal desires above everything else. Unsurprisingly we find a similar trait in our local churches. People want quick answers to their questions and fiery prayers that will bail them out of any challenge or predicament. One of the ways by which some do this is to go into fasting – with the mindset that fasting automatically guarantees and accelerates answers to prayer. Consequently, fasting is being greatly abused in the church today, with lots of Christians fasting for the wrong purposes.

WRONG MOTIVES FOR FASTING

There are people who have turned fasting to fashion – they fast simply to show off that they are spiritual. Jesus warns against this practice by stating that such fasting exercise will not get God's attention. Matthew 6:16-17 states, "Moreover, when you fast, do not be like the hypocrites, with a sad countenance. For they disfigure their faces that they may appear to men to be fasting. Assuredly, I say to you, they have their reward. But you, when you fast, anoint your head and wash your face, so that you do not appear to men to be fasting, but to your Father who is in the secret place; and your Father who sees in secret will reward you openly."

Fasting by believers is strictly for the purpose of humbling the soul before God, rather than to show-off to men. The Jewish practice was to smear ashes on the face and wear grim expressions during times of fasting. While these acts originally expressed true repentance, hypocrites soon adopted them as a mark of false piety. The fact that Christ used "when", rather than "if" means that fasting is expected to be a regular practice for believers, rather than an optional one.

Again, there are those who fast with the primary intention of manipulating, arm-twisting or compelling God to respond to their prayer instantly by fire! Yet, the truth is that fasting does not change God. The purpose of fasting is to change human beings and to bring our flesh under subjection, so that our spirit body can rise above the flesh. Hebrews 13:8-9 states, "Jesus Christ is the same yesterday, today, and forever. Do not be carried about with various and strange doctrines. For it is good that the heart be established by grace, not with foods which have not profited those who have been occupied with them."

Christians should remember that Christ is always the same and, thus, we must judge every teaching according to the gospel.

FASTING EXPLAINED

So, what is fasting? Fasting is a valuable spiritual force; it is abstinence from food and drink for a defined period to enable you concentrate on God. Our Lord Jesus characteristically fasted very often during His earthly ministry. A notable event marked the 40 days fast he had at the beginning of His ministry. His disciples, though, did not fast when Jesus was on earth. Matthew 9:14-15 explains, stating, "Then the disciples of John came to Him, saying, "Why do we and the Pharisees fast often, but Your disciples do not fast?" And Jesus said to them, "Can the friends of the bridegroom mourn as long as the bridegroom is with them? But the days will come when the bridegroom will be taken away from them, and then they will fast."

The meaning of this verse is that we must fast right now. The presence of the Messiah gave the disciples an irrepressible joy that was inconsistent with fasting. There are two different types of fasting: (1) Personal fasting by the individual believer; (2) corporate fasting, such as fasting called by the church or a fellowship group.

WHY WE MUST FAST

1. Fasting is a way of humbling ourselves before the Lord to enable us focus our total attention on Him. King David in Psalm 35:12-14, states, "They reward

me evil for good, to the sorrow of my soul. But as for me, when they were sick, my clothing was sackcloth; I humbled myself with fasting; and my prayer would return to my own heart. I paced about as though he were my friend or brother; I bowed down heavily, as one who mourns for his mother."

2. Fasting is a way of disciplining our body, so that our spirit can connect with God, since we subject flesh and blood to the Holy Spirit.

3. Fasting deals with doubts and unbelief to a good extent. The right way of fasting involves withdrawing temporarily from physical things and some regular habits so that we can spend more time studying and meditating on the word. This must be supported by fervent prayer at a chosen interval of time during this period, based on individual or corporate scheduled agreement.

Fasting without some purposeful withdrawal from regular transactions and the hullabaloos of the environment will minimize the impacts of our concentration and its effectiveness on the purpose of our fasting. Romans 8:5-7 states, "For those who live according to the flesh set their minds on the things of the flesh, but those who live according to the Spirit, the things of the Spirit. For to be carnally minded is death, but to be spiritually minded is life and peace.

Because the carnal mind is enmity against God; for it is not subject to the law of God, nor indeed can be."

Paul described two different kinds of existence or two "mind-sets" and two different outcomes - the old and the new. Unregenerate people are hostile to God and are unable to submit to God's law because they lack God's spirit, which makes submission possible.

4. Believers fast when we are desperately seeking God's intervention for troubling challenges and occurrences in our lives. These may include our finances, healing from infirmities, difficult and disobedient children, marriage issues of our children and even friends, divisions in our church, and so forth.

5. Fasting can transform our prayer life into a richer and more rewarding experience. It involves a lifestyle of thanksgiving, mostly thanking God in our prayers in bigger proportion to habitually asking; and maturity to a level where we pray much more for others than for ourselves.

NOTABLE BIBLICAL EXAMPLES OF FASTING

1. Our Lord Jesus fasted for 40 days, after which the heavens opened unto Him. Matthew 4:1-4 states, "Then Jesus was led up by the Spirit into the wilderness to be tempted by the devil. And when He had fasted forty days and forty nights, afterward He was hungry. Now when the tempter came to Him, he said, "If You are the Son of God, command that these stones become bread." But He answered and said, "It is written, Man shall not live by bread alone, but by every word that proceeds from the mouth of God.'"

The temptation of Christ highlights numerous parallels between Jesus and Old Testament Israel. Deuteronomy 8:2-3 says that the Lord led Israel into the wilderness to be tested for 40 years. Similarly, Jesus was led into the wilderness to be tested for 40 days. The three temptations Jesus faced parallel the tests Israel faced in the wilderness, and every scripture that Jesus quoted in response to his temptations was drawn from God's message to the Israelites about their wilderness test (Deuteronomy 6-8). Israel failed its tests, while Jesus passed His and thereby fulfilled all righteousness (Matthew 3:15). Thus, He qualified to create a new spiritual Israel. He later chose 12 disciples to parallel Israel's 12 tribes and identified His followers as the new Israel.

The fact that Jesus was naturally hungry shows that He was truly human as well as divine. Jesus aimed to end His fast when the test was over and no sooner. God would signal the end by providing food. Matthew 4:11 shows that at the fast's end, angels came and ministered to Jesus. Israel failed to trust God to provide food and water during their wilderness wanderings. However, the embodiment of the new Israel had unwavering trust in God's care (Matthew 3:17). God's words are not idle, but are to be received as commands. While Deuteronomy 8:1 teaches that man lives by following God's commandments, the Lord taught that obeying God is more important than being well-fed. Israel struggled to learn this truth (Exodus 16:3; Numbers 11:4-5). In contrast, Jesus hungered for righteousness more than bread and thirsted for obedience more than water, therefore he urged His disciples to have the same priority (Matthew 5:6).

2. Moses fasted for 40 days twice, and the covenant was renewed between God and Israel. Exodus 34:27-28 states, "Then the Lord said to Moses, "Write these words, for according to the tenor of these words I have made a covenant with you and with Israel." So he was there with the Lord forty days and forty nights; he neither ate bread nor drank water. And He wrote on the tablets the words of the covenant, the Ten Commandments."

3. Elijah fasted for 40 days, an episode that happened after he had escaped from Jezebel who had threatened to kill him the following day. 1 Kings 19:7-8 says, "And the angel of the Lord came back the second time, and touched him, and said, "Arise and eat, because the journey is too great for you." So he arose, and ate and drank; and he went in the strength of that food forty days and forty nights as far as Horeb, the mountain of God." God's miraculous provision was resumed purely for Prophet Elijah. After Elijah had eaten and rested, he returned to the place where the covenant had been given, Mount Horeb, or Sinai, where his personal faith was also nourished.

4. Queen Esther called for three days fast for herself and the Jews to avert imminent disaster being set up to exterminate all Jews, by Haman who had access to the king. Esther 4:14-16 narrates, "For if you remain completely silent at this time, relief and deliverance will arise for the Jews from another place, but you and your father's house will perish. Yet who knows whether you have come to the kingdom for such a time as this?" Then Esther told them to reply to Mordecai: "Go, gather all the Jews who are present in Shushan, and fast for me; neither eat nor drink for three days, night or day. My maids and I will fast likewise. And so I will go to the king, which is against the law; and if I perish, I perish!"

Mordecai and Esther would regard relief and deliverance as attributable to God's providential care for His people, whatever the source from whom it ultimately emerged. This conclusion is evidenced by Mordecai's famous suggestion that Esther had come to the kingdom for such a time as this. The implication is that God had a destiny for Esther, since all the concurrent events in the last four years had put her in this position for this very purpose and moment.

This fast here was unusually long, highlighting the severity of the threat to the Jewish people. The good news is that Esther won the king's favor, ending the persecution of the Jews; while Haman, the evil plotter, was hung by the ropes he had prepared for the Jews. Hallelujah!

5. Daniel had 21 days of partial fast in other to seek the face of God for his people in Babylon. Daniel 10:2-3 states, "In those days I, Daniel, was mourning three full weeks. I ate no pleasant food, no meat or wine came into my mouth, nor did I anoint myself at all, till three whole weeks were fulfilled."

Daniel had been mourning because of the poor conditions of the returned captives. The Samaritans were opposing reconstruction of the temple, which had stopped the work (Ezra 4:5,24). Daniel engaged in a semi-fast, not because the food had been offered to idols (Daniel 1:8) but to enable him focus and give priority to prayer.

DARE TO FAST!

The major types of fasting include personal fasting and corporate fasting, usually called by a group, church, or a fellowship life group. Depending on the leading of the Holy Spirit, fasting without eating or taking water, juices or liquids can be on for days. The bottom-line is to ensure that you study the word and pray more during fasting, failure of which will turn the fast to a mere hunger strike.

All the essential guidelines discussed should be managed together to achieve life-changing fasting rounds. Fasting is an essential tool for the believer to temper the inescapable storms of life, especially in the areas of healing, deliverance, and pulling down of strongholds.

When done in the appropriate way, fasting can be very rewarding for your spiritual growth. It is very pertinent and essential for you to set aside regular days of the week or month to withdraw from day to day pressures of work and home to seek the face of God.

Chapter 11

NECESSITY OF TRUE REPENTANCE

"True repentance is no light matter. It is a thorough change of heart about sin, a change showing itself in godly sorrow and humiliation – in heartfelt confession before the throne of grace – in a complete breaking off from sinful habits, and an abiding hatred of all sin."
–J.C. Ryle

In these days of mere "prosperity" and "feel-good" sermons, there is an urgent need to revisit this cardinal doctrine of the Bible, which not only frequently featured in the sermons of Christ Himself but became a crucial foundation stone for building the early church. Despite being the most loving teacher and best motivational preacher ever in history, Christ never shied away from telling the people, "unless you repent you will all likewise perish" (Luke 13:5). And as He was about to ascend to heaven, He made this message of repentance to be the central component of the Great Commission handed over to His followers (Luke 24:47). The apostles on their part ensured to keep to the mandate – as we find throughout the book of Acts; and we, the church at this crucial moment, cannot afford to be silent about it.

Let me begin the exposition on this doctrine by establishing this basic truth – true repentance goes beyond sorrow for sin, remorse for being caught in wrong behavior or, more commonly, emotional outbursts driven by fear, guilt or shame. People sometimes get emotional during a spirited or convicting sermon and we tend to consider this a sign of repentance in response to the conviction of the Holy Spirit. The truth, however, is that true repentance is not a mere emotional outburst; rather it is a conscious decision to move in a completely new direction.

What this implies, therefore, is that it is quite easy and possible that a person displays great emotion by shedding crocodile tears and demonstrating some other physical reactions, without really repenting biblically. Repentance is an inner change of mind, resulting in an outward change of turning around completely. It involves a deliberate decision or resolve to run from sins by intentionally changing one's mind and surrendering one's heart and life to the Savior.

Matthew 3:1-3 says of the message of John the Baptist, "In those days John the Baptist came preaching in the wilderness of Judea, and saying, "Repent, for the kingdom of heaven is at hand!" For this is he who was spoken of by the prophet Isaiah, saying: "The voice of one crying in the wilderness: Prepare the way of the Lord; Make His paths straight".

John's message focused on repentance and the coming of the Kingdom of heaven. Jesus emphasized the same thing at the outset of His ministry (Matthew 4:17). The Kingdom is defined as the rule that God exercises through the person, work, and teachings of Jesus. The call to repentance is an appeal to us that we must abandon sinful lifestyles and express sorrow and total rejection of sins.

As I mentioned earlier, the early apostles faithfully kept to the message of repentance. Peter, in Acts 3:19-21, proclaims, "Repent therefore and be converted, that your sins may be blotted out, so that times of refreshing may come from the presence of the Lord, and that He may send Jesus Christ, who was preached to you before, whom heaven must receive until the times of restoration of all things, which God has spoken by the mouth of all His holy prophets since the world began."

Peter called on his listeners to repent and be forgiven

on the basis of what he had said about who Jesus was, how He was treated by the Jewish people, and how God had vindicated Him by raising Him from the dead. Early Christians looked with expectation to the second coming of Jesus and the restoration of all things that accompany the establishment of His earthly kingdom. God had foretold this through the prophets, starting as far back as Moses.

We must, therefore, understand that if there is no repentance, there can be no releasing of the time of refreshing from the presence of the Lord.

WHY REPENTANCE?

1. Repentance is the first requirement for genuine salvation.

True repentance must always precede true faith, without which our profession of faith is an empty declaration. Many believers today are insecure, unstable and always wavering in doubts and unbelief, due to this particular reason. They profess faith, while they have never really repented of their sins or confessed their trespasses. The faith they profess consequently procures for them neither the favor of God nor the respect of the world. 2 Corinthians 7:9-10 states, "Now I rejoice, not that you were made sorry, but that your sorrow led to repentance. For you were made sorry in a godly manner, that you might suffer loss from us in nothing. For godly sorrow produces repentance leading to salvation, not to be regretted; but the sorrow of the world produces death." Again, we find a scriptural order of repentance and faith in Acts 2:38-39, which states, "Then Peter said to them, "Repent, and let every one of you be baptized in the name of Jesus Christ for the remission of sins; and you shall receive the gift of the Holy Spirit. For the promise is to you and to your children, and to all who are afar off, as many as the Lord our God will call."

Peter's answer to the crowd indicates three major components in conversion. These include repentance, which means turning around from sin; being baptized publicly in the name of Jesus, which declares repentance and faith, plus it symbolically identifies us with the death, burial, and resurrection of Christ. The gift of the Holy Spirit is a divine favor and seal of conversion, empowering the believer for the life of faith.

Luke 24:46-47 says, "Then He said to them, "Thus it is written, and thus it was necessary for the Christ to suffer and to rise from the dead the third day, and that repentance and remission of sins should be preached in His name to all nations, beginning at Jerusalem." Old Testament (OT) passages that clearly prophesy the suffering of Christ are Psalm 22 and Isaiah 53. A key OT passage for the Messiah's resurrection is Psalm 16:10, also cited several times in the NT.

OT passages that Jesus may have had in mind about repentance being preached to all nations beginning at Jerusalem are Isaiah 2:1-4 and 49:6. Luke 24:27 is Luke's version of the Great commission (Matthew 28:19; Mark 16:15; John 20:21-22).

2. Repentance is very crucial in the life of the believer. (John 21:15-17; Luke 22:62; Psalm 139:23-24).

Any known sin must cause the Christian to take immediate action of repentance; otherwise he will be subjected to degradation and experience spiritual decline. Repentance is an essential and foundational "ritual" that a true believer must address and never sideline. We must regularly invite God to search our lives to examine if there are attitudes, relationships, or activities that need to be expunged out of our lives to free us from the bondage and stronghold of sins.

The example of Peter demonstrates that he was not only remorseful but was totally repentant after repeatedly denying Christ. His life changed permanently, and there is no record in scripture of him ever denying the Lord again, even when he was persecuted and later threatened with death. In other words, Peter genuinely repented and turned his life around and never committed that sin again. That is true repentance.

Here is the full account of what happened to Peter. Luke 22:60-62 states, "But Peter said, "Man, I do not know what you are saying!" Immediately, while he was still speaking, the rooster crowed. And the Lord turned and looked at Peter. Then Peter remembered the word of the Lord, how He had said to him, "Before the rooster crows, you will deny Me three times." So Peter went out and wept bitterly."

Peter denied three years of discipleship in a period of only slightly an hour. Jesus had very recently predicted this event (Luke 22:31-34), and when the rooster crowed after Peter's denials, Jesus turned and looked at him. Peter immediately remembered Jesus' prophecy and wept tears of shame and regret.

However, Jesus restored in Peter in John 21: 15-17 which states, "So when they had eaten breakfast, Jesus said to Simon Peter, "Simon, son of Jonah, do you love Me more than these?" He said to Him, "Yes, Lord; You know that I love You." He said to him, "Feed My lambs." He said to him again a second time, "Simon, son of Jonah, do you love Me?" He said to Him, "Yes, Lord; You know that I love You." He said to him, "Tend My sheep." He said to him the third time, "Simon, son of Jonah, do you love Me?" Peter was grieved because He said to him the third time, "Do you love Me?""

Peter had denied Jesus three times (John 18:15-18, 25-27); now Jesus asked him three times to reaffirm his love for him before recommissioning him for the gospel work. In Psalm 139:23-24, the Psalmist pleads, "Search me, O God, and know my heart; Try me, and know my anxieties; And see if there is any wicked way in me, And lead me in the way everlasting.". The psalmist submitted his thoughts and motives to the Lord's scrutiny, asking God to reveal any wicked way in him.

ULTIMATE PRACTICAL EXAMPLE OF TRUE REPENTANCE (LUKE 15:11-32)

Perhaps the best example and demonstration of true repentance is revealed in the parable of the lost son (The Prodigal Son). The story narrates how the younger of two brothers went afar off into a distant land, after forcefully getting his share of his father's inheritance and virtually turning his back on his family and home. He recklessly wasted all his inheritance claims on riotous living. He finally ended up wasting all he had in sin and dissipation and lost everything. Eventually, he turned very wretched, hungry, lonely and in rags, sitting and feeding among swine, longing for something to fill his stomach and barely surviving.

Suddenly, and at this point in time, he made a resolve,

saying, "I will arise and go to my father" (Luke 15:18). He did not stop there; he immediately implemented his decision. "And he arose and came to his father" (Luke 15:20).

That lost son apparently displayed true repentance, which involves first the inward decision, then the outward execution of the decision by going back to his father and his home. You may compare his story with yours. How is your relationship with the Heavenly Father currently? Is it cordial or have you gone to "a far country", even though you still attend church regularly or even serve as a worker? Now, is the time to return, before the enemy does more damage to your life.

REPENTANCE IS STILL RELEVANT!

A crucial prerequisite to be truly born again is repentance, without which there can be no salvation of the soul. If a believer does not take adequate concerted action to repent of any known sin, he or she will experience spiritual decline. However, if he honestly and humbly repents and confesses his sins, he will continuously enjoy God's favor, and always have victory and dominion in all areas of life. The choice is ours to make, but we must remember that each choice has its consequences.

CHAPTER 12

LIFE'S INESCAPABLE STORMS AND GOD'S FAITHFULNESS

"Our need is not to prove God's faithfulness but to demonstrate our own, by trusting Him both to determine and to supply our needs according to His will." –JOHN MACARTHUR

The lives of believers can be likened to a building, since we face certain storms from season to season. While the storms hit and last, what will keep the building of our lives standing is a mix of the quality of our foundation, and the quality of the materials with which we have built over the years.

As beloved children of God, who are in constant warfare with life's battles and the enemy's attacks, we must always be prepared to withstand the inevitable challenges and storms of life in the process of our pilgrimage. In this regard, we are expected to always utilize and follow the word of God, build our faith on a solid foundation, pray, and always be led by the Spirit of God.

Cheeringly, God has equipped us to reign over life's storms, tests, trials, and temptations by rooting us in the solid foundation of Christ, while in partnership and fellowship with Him. Storms may come to us as tests in life to strengthen us or facilitate growth in our faith. In fact, if you are never tested or tried with challenges, it is likely that you are not growing in faith or not even walking by faith, because without some kind of test, you simply can be complacent, and start walking by sight.

GOD CANNOT LIE

Regardless of whatever storm you may face or may be currently facing, a sure anchor you can hold on to for strength, stability and safety is the abiding faithfulness of God to every one of His promises to you. Numbers 23:19 says, "God is not a man, that He should lie, nor a son of man, that He should repent. Has He said, and will He not do? Or has He spoken, and will He not make it good?" The New Living Translation says, "God is not a man, so He does not lie. He is not human, so He does not change His mind. Has He ever spoken and failed to act? Has He ever promised and not carried it through?"

We serve a truly dependable God. He has no limitations in terms of time, space, power or authority, since He is sovereign. He is omnipresent, omniscient and omnipotent. Whatever He says therefore, is the absolute TRUTH. Human beings may tell lies, pervert issues, or try to hide the facts, but God is not a man and lying is not at all in His character. He is only capable of telling the truth and the truth is His word, rather than our feelings, emotions, experiences or people's opinions.

This is the more reason you should be familiar with His words generally and His promises for you, in particular. Anytime you are declaring these words, you are agreeing with what God says and thinks for you – thoughts of peace and not of evil (Jeremiah 29:11). And so shall it be for you.

The knowledge that God says exactly what He means is reassuring in that it eliminates any trace of confusion. 2 Peter 1:19 states, "And so we have the prophetic word confirmed, which you do well to heed as a light that shines in a dark place, until the day dawns and the morning star rises in your hearts."

The prophetic scriptures affirmed the apostolic witness that the scriptures act as a torch that shines in a dark world, exposing the dirt and defilement of sin, as well as the lies of Satan and his agents, making it easy to conquer them. We all are expected to live by the scriptures' "torch-light" until the day dawns, that is, until Christ's return.

HOW TO APPLY GOD'S TRUTH TO YOUR LIFE

1. Accept that every promise in God's word is the unequivocal truth.

Settle it in your mind that there is no contradiction in God's word, and that every promise in God's word is the absolute truth. Psalm 103:3 says that God is the one "Who forgives all your iniquities, Who heals all your diseases." By settling it in your heart that there is no contradiction in His word, you must affirm that God does not make us sick. He is indeed our healer, Hallelujah!

Also, Philippians 4:19 says, "And my God shall supply all your need according to His riches in glory by Christ Jesus." You just need to believe, trust, and keep confessing God promises which are true forever! Always declare, profess, and confess God's promises in anticipation of fulfillment.

2. **Never allow your circumstances or feelings to have pre-eminence over what God says.**

Never waver, doubt, or allow unbelief to the extent that your circumstances or feelings have pre-eminence over what God says. Sickness may be attacking the body, but does not override the truth, that "by His stripes you were healed". (Isaiah 53:5; 1 Peter 2:24). 1 Peter 2:24 states, "who Himself bore our sins in His own body on the tree, that we, having died to sins, might live for righteousness—by whose stripes you were healed." You must keep continue to declare and act on what God says as the truth, and ultimately what God says will prevail over all negative feelings and emotions (2 Corinthians 4:18).

3. **Fire up your faith!**

You need to activate your faith always since it is the spiritual force with which we receive from God and resist the fiery darts of the adversary. Romans 10:17 says, "So then faith comes by hearing, and hearing by the word of God." You must, therefore, keep declaring what God says, so that your faith can increase and consequently receive what God has promised, because He cannot lie.

Concerning the effect of faith on prayer, James 5:14-16 states, "Is anyone among you sick? Let him call for the elders of the church, and let them pray over him, anointing him with oil in the name of the Lord. And the prayer of faith will save the sick, and the Lord will raise him up. And if he has committed sins, he will be forgiven. Confess your trespasses to one another, and pray for one another, that you may be healed. The effective, fervent prayer of a righteous man avails much.".

Real healing from any infirmity – physical, spiritual, emotional, financial, marital or professional – is best obtained through prayer of faith. Prayer is not magical incantation or a guarantee of healing, but when offered fervently by a righteous person, God will respond in a way that fits His good purposes. James cites a biblical personality, Elijah, a mere man, who prayed effectively ,bringing answers from heaven by fire. The illustration is intended to show-case a classical example and role-model of an effective prayer to encourage us that our prayers could lead to similar results.

4. Declare your victory.

Jesus, in Mark 11:24 says, "Therefore I say to you, whatever things you ask when you pray, believe that you receive them, and you will have them." The implication is that by confessing that you receive what God promises, you are aligning yourself with God's plan. 1 John 5:14-15 further says, "Now this is the confidence that we have in Him, that if we ask anything according to His will, He hears us. And if we know that He hears us, whatever we ask, we know that we have the petitions that we have asked of Him."

The deepest assurance in prayer is to know that God hears us. Knowing this is to have what we have asked Him for. Prayer seeks communion of believers with the Father, rather than acquisition of favors or satisfaction of worldly desires. You are aligning yourself with God's plan by confessing that you have received what God promises. Saying the contrary, dictated by your feelings or circumstances, negates God's plans and will not make prayer work as desired.

Proverbs 18:20-21 states, "A man's stomach shall be satisfied from the fruit of his mouth; From the produce of his lips he shall be filled. Death and life are in the power of the tongue, And those who love it will eat its fruit." The approach a person takes in his speech will return to him. Once you believe, then keep trusting, declaring and confessing what you believe, not what you feel.

5. Accept the authority of God's word.

2 Timothy 3:16 says, "All Scripture is given by inspiration of God, and is profitable for doctrine, for reproof, for correction, for [a]instruction in righteousness." The scriptures could lead you to "know the truth" (2 Timothy 2:25; 1 Timothy 2:4). They have the power

to strengthen and increase your faith. However, the practical effectiveness of God's word on your life is heavily weighted on your response to it. You will ever receive spiritual and all-round nourishment while you feed on the word with meekness and sincerity. 1 Peter 2:1-2 says, "Therefore, laying aside all malice, all deceit, hypocrisy, envy, and all evil speaking, as newborn babes, desire the pure milk of the word, that you may grow thereby."

As a matter of discipline, allegiance and obedience, resolve by yourself to get into the word. Study and meditate on it continually for progressive nourishment, development, and growth. You cannot please God without faith (Hebrews 11:6), and faith comes by hearing God's word (Romans 10:17).

The reason why so little faith is rampant among many professing Christians today is because they do not devote quality time to studying and meditating on the word. You can choose to be different – to be a man or woman of faith, power and authority with God and man by giving maximum priority to the word in all areas of your life.

YOU ARE IN SAFE HANDS!

Certainly, every word of God is a "sure" word – 2 Peter 1:19. The knowledge that God says what He means and means what He says is a very good thing, because it eliminates any trace of doubt or confusion. Believers must therefore follow, abide and live by the leading of the scriptures in the Bible, and refuse to allow their emotions, feelings, or circumstances of life to take pre-eminence. We must not be declaring our feelings or emotions. Change for the better comes as we change our confessions to what God says in harmony with His promises, while in alignment with His purposes for our lives.

LIST OF REFERENCES

Ken Blanchard and Spence Johnson: The One Minute Manager", the #1 Motivator of People is feedback on results

Finis Jennings Dake: God's Plan for Man – Revealing God's Perfect Plan for All Creation, Dake Publishing Inc. 2010

Mark Dever: Nine Marks of a Healthy Church, Crossway Publishing, 2013

A.L. Joyce Crill: Supernatural Living Through the Gifts of the Holy Spirit, Powerhouse Publishing, 1995

Holman Study Bible NKJV Edition, 2015, Comprehensive Study

Douglas McGregor – The Massachusetts Institute of Technology (MIT): Two Contrasting Views on Motivation

Merriam Webster Dictionary

Charles Stanley: Success God's Way

Kenneth Hagin: The Triumphant Church – Dominion Over All Powers

RCCG Living Word Chapel (LWC): Bible Study Notes Year 2004 to Date

Rick Warren: Be in Constant Communion with God, 2014

Andrew Womack: Staying Full of God. http//:www.sermoncentral.com/sermons

John Piper: The Absolute Sovereignty of God, What is Roman Nine About?

Vincentia Ministries, Kenya, 2018, In Constant Communion with God.

www.ingramcontent.com/pod-product-compliance
Lightning Source LLC
Chambersburg PA
CBHW060738100426
42742CB00028B/2125